tarot basics

tarot basics

a guide to using & interpreting the cards

JOHANNES FIEBIG & EVELIN BÜRGER

STERLING ETHOS
New York

STERLING ETHOS
New York

STERLING ETHOS and the distinctive Sterling Ethos logo are registered trademarks of Sterling Publishing Co., Inc.

Text © 2006 by Johannes Fiebig and Evelin Bürger

ISBN 978-1-4549-5257-2
ISBN 978-1-4549-5258-9 (e-book)

For information about custom editions, special sales, and premium purchases, please contact specialsales@unionsquareandco.com.

Printed in India

2   4   6   8   10   9   7   5   3   1

unionsquareandco.com

Cover and interior design by Stacy Wakefield Forte
Image credits: Shutterstock.com: Prachaya Roekdeethaweesab: cover, 2, 5 (hand/frame); 202; Valedi: 13, 23, 31, 48, 49, 61, 228, 229; Wonder-studio: 6

CONTENTS

INTRODUCTION

ALL MEANINGS are obvious. Sometimes they may be an "elusive obvious," as Moshé Feldenkrais put it. But this is why we can start with the tarot without knowing anything about it. And why we shall discover even more aspects and new sights of the pictures only later, once we are acquainted with them. This book, *Tarot Basics*, aims to offer a path to understanding the cards that is alert, empathic, and enhances your knowledge by experience. Anyone can use the tarot, simply by realizing what he or she is seeing, applying the knowledge at hand, and exploring the present significance.

THE TRICKY THING CALLED MEANING

As Arthur E. Waite himself pointed out, "The true tarot is symbolism; it speaks no other language and offers no other signs."

Tarot symbols and pictures include more than just one message. They tell numerous stories and continue to tell new stories each time you encounter them. They offer multiple perspectives of perception and interpretation. This is the main difference between an authentic tarot deck and other kinds of illustrations, card games, and comic designs, which may be fantastic and full of imagination, but do not refer to the specific characteristics of the tarot. The two classics of the tarot—the decks of Waite-Smith and of Crowley-Harris—demonstrate this, which is why we have highlighted them in this book, in addition to the Marseille, which dates back to the seventeenth and eighteenth centuries. But any deck that adheres to multilayered tarot symbolism can be interpreted in this way.

IMAGES THAT ALLOW AND REQUEST A SECOND SIGHT

The typical modern tarot presents a double perception for each card. For example, when you look at the image of The Emperor in the Waite-Smith deck, you see a stony desert. The card shows a wasteland.

The stony desert, the wasteland from the picture of The Emperor, Waite-Smith Tarot

This may represent the lack, or maybe the loss, of fecundity. It can stand for a kind of power, order, or government that does not let anything grow. The same picture could demonstrate the very beginning of cultivation: The challenge and the ability to "turn a desert into a garden" as is typical for the early springtime in the month of Aries (in the northern hemisphere). This echoes scripture quoted in Christian Easter ceremonies. Several heads of an Aries and an Easter lamb are depicted in the respective pictures of the Waite-Smith and the Crowley-Harris Tarots.

In one perception, the Emperor symbolizes the cropless end of a rule hostile to life. In another perception, the picture highlights our potency to create and develop new fruitful life, also in respect to the individual question currently concerned.

DOUBLE MEANING OF PICTORIAL DETAILS

Foot on the water from the picture of The Star, Waite-Smith Tarot

Another example: The foot of the "Star" woman is placed on the water surface.

In the language of symbols, "water" means psyche, soul, and feelings. The "foot on the water" again provides a double meaning: one is positive—the water supports (it is carrying the woman in the picture); in other words, psyche and faith provide a basis and a "standpoint" upon which we can navigate the world. In terms of a negative meaning, in water, there is no access to feelings. One is not able to enter the water. We stand at the shore as if our soul was frozen, emotions numbed.

Similarly, within the Crowley-Harris Tarot, the "Five of Cups" is the only card in that suit that presents all cups completely empty.

This may point to inner emptiness, emotional ebbs, or spiritual deficiency. This meaning would warn against continuing on the current path. On the other hand, the same symbolism demonstrates the biggest possible *openness* and receptiveness for something new. The latter may apply to moments in our life when we experience a great change. The old has gone, and the new is still to come. This meaning would encourage you to trust and to go ahead.

HOW DO WE DEAL WITH MULTIPLE MEANINGS?

At first, make sure that you see encouraging and warning pros and cons within each card. For some pictures, this is quite easy. For others it takes a bit of investigation and self-exploration.

The warning and encouraging meanings may be valid simultaneously. For example, the Five of Cups above may warn us against emotional or mental exhaustion, and simultaneously it may encourage us to be open to new emotional or mental experiences.

This book was conceived to present basic hints about how to successfully deal with the numerous dimensions of these meaningful pictures, so as you read it you will learn how to interpret the rest of the cards in the deck.

PICTURES LEADING TO MINDFULNESS

Whether or not the cups are filled; whether they are standing upright or have been tilted; whether some flowers or other plants are rooted in the earth or are hovering—each detail may be a hint, or a trigger to your personal approach to the respective card—and a key to the personal meaning.

The Five of Cups, the only card showing just empty cups in the Crowley-Harris Tarot

From top to bottom, birds in the four Swords court cards, Waite-Smith Tarot—the Queen, the King, the Knight, and the Page of Swords

introduction

⋮

10

Through the pictures of the four Swords court cards in the Waite-Smith Tarot, the depicted birds tell a story, or diverse stories, illustrated by their quantity and the configuration.

Also consider that a white horse appears five times within the imagery of the Waite-Smith Tarot. And if you have once made up your mind about what this symbol could mean, you may transfer this to each of the five respective pictures, thus getting support for your personal interpretation by the composition of the card symbols.

Such an artful and mindful creation of the imagery—with clear and consistent lines of symbolic themes and details—is something special. It is a mark of a special high quality. According to our experience, the Waite-Smith Tarot and the Crowley-Harris Thoth Tarot are doing best in this respect (and the same is valid for the Dalí Tarot in another unique way).

NO HIDDEN MEANINGS

Here is another example of the symbolic richness of the pictures, one more of the Crowley-Harris Thoth Tarot. The stalks and the roots in the pictures of the "cup" cards tell a multitude of stories.

Look, for example, at the picture of the Three of Cups: The stalks/hoses build a perfect water cycle. (That can mean a pleasant "round thing" in terms of spiritual wholeness and personal integrity. But it may also demonstrate a spiritual captivity, again and again repeating certain feelings and emotions. So, you can apply the positive meaning, and omit the card's negative aspects, as a chance or a challenge in your real life.)

Roots are the theme in the picture of the Four of Cups: Here, and only in this picture, the rootage can be fully recognized. This fact may be interpreted in multiple ways.

In the Five of Cups, the news is quite different: Here, and only in this picture, all cups are empty. This may indicate either a problem or a good chance, as explained before. It is a picture of change and transformation in the realm of the cups (which correspond to soul, emotion, and spirituality). This interpretation derives from the fact that the stems are shaping a butterfly (in the lower part of the picture) and a heart (at the top of the picture).

The Six of Cups displays interwoven stalks. This can represent the complexity of feelings and emotions. There is no end in sight. And again, this may present various aspects of meaning.

A TOOL TO PROVE YOUR BELIEFS

The pictures of the cards are the first and last benchmark when reading and interpretating the cards. Remember Arthur E. Waite's words: The tarot's pictures speak for themselves.

When authors and scholars quote Greek myths, the Kabbalah, or the I Ching in their interpretations of the cards, it underlines that author's or scholar's views. You do not need to study these traditions if you wish to interpret the tarot.

The I Ching has no direct or historic relation to the tarot at all. Connecting its teachings to the cards may be helpful for an author or a scholar to propagate their personal beliefs, but beyond that, there is no proof that the I Ching and the tarot had any direct influence on each other in history.

As for the Greek myths, if you are interested in them, go ahead and study them. There are so many other mythologies, traditional fairy tales, symbolic languages, and techniques such as dream interpretation that may be interesting and helpful, too.

The Kabbalah and the tarot have a more direct link, but not as strong as some have implied. Both have existed for many hundreds of years. In 1856, these two disciplines were combined for the first time by Éliphas Lévi, but no earlier than that. So, for the longest part of its history, the tarot existed without any connection to the Kabbalah at all. Please also note that there are many different

Meaningful rootage: details from the Three of Cups, Four of Cups, Five of Cups, and Six of Cups, from the Crowley-Harris Thoth Tarot

introduction

11

ways to understand and use the Kabbalah. The same is true for astrology, as well as many other traditions.

Study whatever you want and learn whatever may be necessary for you. But do not believe in "gurus." Do not seek to follow in the footsteps of the sage; look for what they sought. You should gravitate toward meanings and intentions that have been proven to work. Strive for a growing understanding of the pictures—for training on a personal level by reading the cards again and again, a practice that will playfully support you checking, confirming, and amending your beliefs with respect to your important questions.

Enjoy the Tarot!
Evelin Bürger & Johannes Fiebig

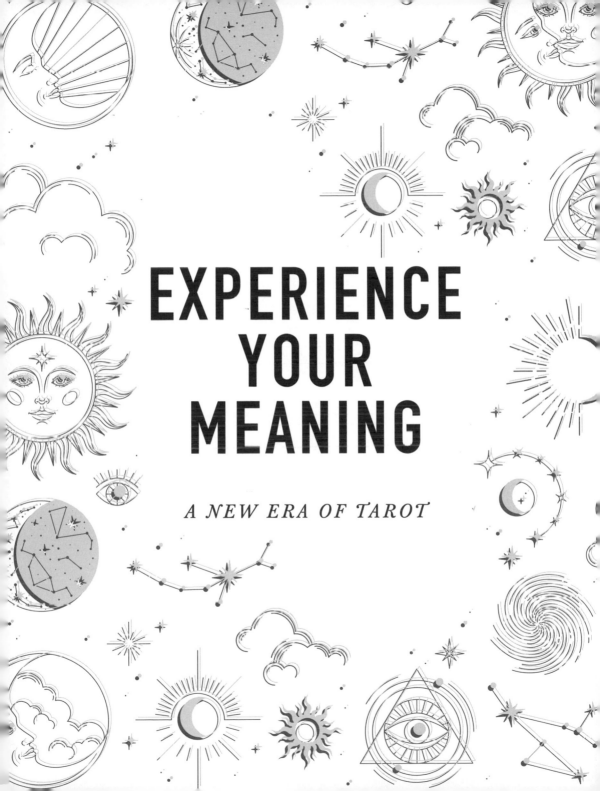

EXPERIENCE YOUR MEANING

A NEW ERA OF TAROT

TAROT IS AN old card game rediscovered in a totally new way. Those who are new to Tarot and want to understand how it works should try comparing it to dream interpretations. Tarot cards contain pictures and symbols that you can use the same way you would use images and symbols from dreams.

Tarot is a proper name, but the word itself does not provide any clue as to its meaning. Tarot refers to a deck of seventy-eight cards divided into specific sections and suits.

The first Tarot cards date from the Renaissance. Between circa 1430 and 1460, artists in Milan and Bologna and other Italian places painted them for royalty. The Renaissance was a time of rebirth and transition. People were eager to leave the Middle Ages behind. They rediscovered and revived countless traditions of antiquity. The choices of the motifs in Tarot are a mirror of the spirit of the Renaissance. The seventy-eight Tarot cards allude to the many different cultural eras of history from the Renaissance through the Middle Ages to the ancient Greeks and Romans, as well as the early Egyptians and Babylonians.

PART OF A CULTURAL TURN

Today in America and Europe, millions of people use Tarot cards in a way that has little to do with the well-known old-fashioned type of fortune-telling. And it all started with the hippies. The human potential movement during the 1960s unearthed many things from the past and brought new ideas and awareness to the Western world. For instance, the "people in motion" of those times rediscovered traditions, philosophies, and ideas, such as Hermann Hesse and Carl Gustav Jung, Zen Buddhism, the Chinese I Ching, and last but not least, Tarot cards. In 1976, Bob Dylan used the image of the "III–The Empress" card from the Waite-Smith deck on the back cover of his *Desire* album. During this same period, millions of people came in contact with Tarot cards.

Soon after, the women's movement was responsible for the popularity of today's distinct, modern form of Tarot. Since the 1980s, many newspapers and magazines have done stories on Tarot. In fact, Tarot is now a part of our culture.

LOVE, DEATH, AND THE DEVIL

Tarot represents the magic of "the moment" and deals with the confrontation of "chance." In this sense, "the moment," understood as an event in time, plays a very important role. In practical terms, the emphasis is on personal perception, insight, and awareness.

At least three essential sources nurture the magic of Tarot: the encounter with cultural and personal motifs, the work with "chance," and personal and specific experiences.

Every one of the seventy-eight cards introduces one or more themes. In particular, the twenty-two cards that make up the Major Arcana invite us to analyze our basic orientation and belief system. The cards of the Major Arcana represent the main stations of life. We encounter love, death, and the devil (see "VI The Lovers," "XIII–Death," and "XV–The Devil" on pp. 75, 89, and 93). Birth, marriage, and death, which form the most important triad of life, also appear in the twenty-two cards of the Major Arcana as "XIX–The Sun," "VI–The Lovers," and "XIII–Death" (see pp. 101, 75, and 89).

In today's world, we seem to have lost our bearings and are full of questions. Tarot can be very useful and healing because it helps us examine our own understanding of love, death, and the devil. We have a chance to visualize what these mean to us in general and, in particular, at the very moment when we put the cards on the table.

We will discover "II–The High Priestess," "0–The Fool," and "IX–The Hermit" within us. Once we sense that "IX–The

*experience
your meaning*

15

Hermit" means that we are capable of relying on ourselves in addition to the traditional view that we have been deserted, we become curious about the deeper meaning of the card. What is the significance of the star and the brilliant diamond in his lamp, and what is he deciding about loneliness or trust?

We can also look at "IV–The Emperor" and "III–The Empress" as the archetypes of the father and the mother. From this, we can explore our personal experiences and deepen our understanding of our roles as men and women and as mothers and fathers.

Interpreting Tarot cards is like going to a school where you can independently explore your way of life. Tarot does not demand that you adhere to any specific worldview. On the contrary, it helps develop your own understanding of the large and small questions of life.

CONSIDERING CHANCE

It is constructive to spend time meditating on the images used in Tarot. "Chance," however, adds a special kind of excitement to laying out the cards. Which card will turn up? As soon as you reveal the card, the "magic of the moment" unfolds, beginning a dialogue between the image and the observer. First you check which card you selected, then you recognize the picture and what it symbolizes, and finally you begin to ponder the message that it conveys.

The appearance of a particular card does not mean that you have found the answer to your question. It is the dialogue, the intimate internal conversation, that eventually produces a clear answer. The more open and free from bias a particular interpretation is, the more room you have for probing the symbolic meanings of a particular image and for determining what the specific message means to you. That which seems to happen by "chance" is the vehicle, the stimulus, for a productive analysis. This explains the intellectual and cultural tradition of Tarot reading, which is different from fortune-telling. We are finding that art and science have influenced today's Tarot, allowing us to see and examine "chance" more productively and creatively.

Fortune-telling gives every card a relatively narrow meaning, which is applied to men and women alike, regardless of time or place. On the other hand, Tarot cards have pictures. We cannot reduce them to one or two examples without losing substance. Pictures and symbols always have a personal and special component that relates to a specific situation.

At the beginning of the twentieth century, art and science began to recognize "chance" as a productive factor, incorporating it in conceptual frameworks. For example, in the arts, the surrealist André Breton talked about emotions "coming from the belly." In jazz and dance, expressionists elevated "chance" to the art of improvisation. Pierre Boulez, one of the fathers of the "new music," used "chance" in compositions and performances. In science, many different systems and game theories, as well as the theory of relativity and probability, used the concept of "chance." Since 1980, all the social sciences have included "chance" in their theories. Thus, we see that "chance" is a relevant, creative factor and a very important part of the reality of life. Tarot did not invent it.

YOUR MIRROR FOR UNDERSTANDING LIFE

The hallmark of the new Tarot is that Tarot is a "mirror." This concept came from the feminist movement of the 1970s. The term mirror implies that personal insight plays a major role in the process. This is the difference between fortune-telling and the new self-exploring techniques, including dream interpretation and reading Tarot cards for yourself. Fortune-telling and old-school oracle techniques don't recognize the individual. Their recipe-like

experience
your meaning

17

interpretations leave no room for the unfolding of personal truth, which must remain at least partially shrouded in secrecy.

Picture the following:

You see the street in front of your house. Many people are moving about on that street. Every person sees this street differently. The physical act of seeing, which depends on each viewer's size, angle of vision, visual acuity, etc., results in very different perceptions of the street.

Experience and attitude also influence perception. An older person sees the street differently from a young person, a woman differently from a man, a happy person differently from an angry person.

Specific interests are further influences on an individual's perception. An individual who simply drives through on the way to another destination sees the street differently from one who lives there. Yet, it is the same street. The street exists and represents an actual, common reference point for all who know it. In that sense, it is not at all relative. At the same time, this street is also a term for any matter, for the world in general.

We need many experiences, personal as well as with others, in order to see all the "different" streets. Only then will we come into our own.

How we perceive a Tarot card or a "street" in everyday life may tell us a lot about our implicit point of view, personal desires and fears, talents, and challenges. Some of these are shared by many people, while others point especially to our unique personalities and illuminate the value of the individual.

TAROT—THE ART OF LIVING

Many people have had good experiences with fortune-telling. They are amazed by how much someone can "read into the cards." The client becomes just as involved in the outcome as the reader is. As a matter of fact, many psychological experiments have shown that the client may read more into the information than he or she would like to, especially in situations that create tension and a sense of apprehension. But fortune-telling and Tarot reading reveal only a small portion of the much larger connections existing in life.

Many people discover this even without consulting a fortune-teller. For instance, a woman vacationing in Italy was suddenly overcome with a feeling that her child in Germany was sick and needed help. When she was unable to reach her home or relatives by phone, she packed her bags and went home. Her premonition was correct. Her daughter was sick and really did need help.

Every time we confront life's larger dimension, we have an opportunity to look into the secrets of fate and chance, of premonition and intuition. Symbolic languages, such as Tarot, offer a way to pursue these secrets.

Many people, however, have had bad experiences with fortune-telling. A fortune-teller told a woman that she would face a severe crisis within the week. The woman was shocked, but she was smart enough to visit three other fortune-tellers that same day. Not one of the others mentioned an impending catastrophe. The week passed with no problems. The only real catastrophe had been the first fortune-teller's outrageous prophecy.

In another case, a man abandoned his wife and little girl. A fortune-teller promised the wife that he would be back by Christmas. December 25 came and went, and she was still sitting and waiting. When he did not show up all the trust she had in the fortune-teller turned to disappointment and despair. Later,

experience
your meaning

⋮

19

she took up Tarot for herself and found it very helpful in dealing with her pain.

A twelve-year-old boy came to visit our house, saw the Tarot cards, and started to go through them. He became very excited and repeatedly commented about the "death card." As it turned out, he had watched a James Bond movie in which Tarot cards were used. In the movie, someone died every time that card appeared. A few words of explanation reassured him. The "death card," however, is one more example of the difference between old-fashioned fortune-telling and the way we presently interpret symbols. Today, the Tarot "XIII–Death" card means you need to finish something; you need to take care of something; or you need to let go of something. The Grim Reaper is the symbol of death and dying, but more than anything else, the reaper wants to harvest. In other words, when you see this card, the question is what do you want to "harvest" during your lifetime.

When we begin to explore the world of symbols on our own, we can use our wishes and fears as guides. Which desires are important and helpful? Which wishes make no sense? Which anxieties should be respected and guarded? Which fears should be forgotten about and released? When the images begin to take on meaning and eventually give us answers, the language of symbols has fulfilled its purpose. It can initiate the process of personal growth and change and offer us effective training in the art of living.

CHOOSING DECKS

Today there are thousands of different Tarot decks. A great many of them are reissues of historical editions, while many others are new creations. Among and above all of these, there are three classics, which also illustrate this book.

WAITE-SMITH DECK

The Waite-Smith Tarot deck, also known as the Rider or Rider-Waite-Smith deck, is the most popular deck. It was created by Arthur E. Waite and Pamela Colman Smith and published in 1909 by the Rider Publishing House in London. This deck is easy to start with. At the same time, professionals find that this deck possesses an incredible depth from which they can work on many different levels.

Today, the Tarot world is almost unthinkable without the Waite-Smith deck. Waite and Smith were masters who condensed the spiritual wisdom and prospects of numerous esoteric, philosophical, and mystical traditions in their images. Because their deck presented pictures on all seventy-eight cards, it was the forerunner of the modern Tarot interpretation, which is based mainly on visual perception. You may want to start out with Waite-Smith cards or choose another deck for comparison and background while keeping a deck of Waite-Smith cards handy. No matter which cards you choose, the Waite-Smith deck provides the best complement.

CROWLEY-HARRIS DECK

After the Waite-Smith deck, the most important version is the Crowley-Harris deck, issued in 1943 by Aleister Crowley and Lady Frieda Harris. However, these cards were not printed until 1969, during the hippie era.

The Crowley-Harris cards incorporate a powerful and artistic use of symbolism. They challenge you and invite you to examine them in a personal way. The literal nature of the way in which Tarot themes are articulated in this deck can be the basis for inspiration and contemplation.

*experience
your meaning*

Aleister Crowley considered himself to be a "black magician." Because of this, people are often apprehensive when viewing his cards. They feel Crowley is not necessarily the person they would want to use as a model. But, as regarding many artists, we have to make a clear distinction between his work and his life. In any case, Crowley cards represent an important and meaningful addition to Tarot.

MARSEILLES DECK

Except for those dating from the Italian Renaissance, Marseilles cards are considered the oldest Tarot cards. They are still an important part of Tarot because many people interested in symbolism have worked with Marseilles cards. Many of the writings based on these cards have been published again. Thus, the Marseilles version plays an important role in today's Tarot.

Taken together, the three versions might be considered the foundation of today's Tarot. Of course, there are many other creative variations. In our discussion of each individual card, we will show illustrations from the Waite-Smith, Crowley-Harris, and Marseilles decks. The interpretation of each individual card (starting on p. 61) refers to the symbols depicted on that card and, in addition, outlines what is typical about each station of the Tarot—for any deck, as long as the deck is more than a mere subjective fantasy and updates the Tarot traditions.

how to
BEGIN

LOOK THROUGH A DECK of Tarot cards. Contemplate the pictures. Select the cards that seem to speak to you.

- ❖ When you are ready, pull your card of the day. To do this, shuffle as you always do. Do not turn the cards over; leave them facedown. Concentrate and pull one card. (We have not included instructions of how to shuffle the deck, how to pull or take a card from the bottom or the top of the deck, or how to put a card on the table, stacked in a pile, fanned out, etc.) The card of the day is not connected to any specific question. Rather, it is meant to be your theme for the day. In a sense, you are elevating one station of Tarot to serve as a magnifying glass for that specific day.

- ❖ Refer to the tables on pages 234 and 235 and find the six Tarot cards of your astrological sign. Now, take your time looking at these six cards or at any one of them individually.

- ❖ Take this opportunity to think about the desires you harbor deep in your heart. This establishes the basic tone you carry as you interpret the Tarot cards for yourself.

As you become familiar with the world of Tarot symbols, you will notice cards that are with and without titles. Remember that a Tarot deck consists of four different groups. Each group has a symbol that appears on every card within the group. The symbols are "Wands," "Cups," "Swords," and "Pentacles (or Disks)." Each group represents a "suit" in a specific color. This does not mean that one particular color belongs to one specific suit. Rather, the color identifies a suit of cards with the same symbol, similar to a conventional deck of cards with hearts, spades, diamonds, and clubs.

These four suits are made up of fifty-six cards. Together, they are called the Minor Arcana. The fifth group consists of the twenty-two cards called the Major Arcana, the "big secret," or the "big stations of Tarot." You will recognize the twenty-two cards of the Major Arcana of a Waite-Smith deck by the number on the top and the subtitle on the bottom of the cards. You can identify the Crowley-Harris cards by the word "Trumps" printed in large, faint letters on each card. Most of the Marseilles cards have a number on the top.

Other versions, including the Crowley-Harris deck, use standard terms, such as "I–The Magician," "IX The Hermit," or "0–The Fool," but they also have subtitles, such as "Success," "Wealth," and "Disappointment." These interpretative titles should not be used by themselves. Do not let them influence you. Until you have more experience, you should cover the subtitles with your thumb, or simply not look at them, as you pull the card.

❖ Go through all seventy-eight cards again. This time, find the one that seems to speak to you or that you like best. Take this card out of the deck. Make a mental note of which one it is and specifically what about it that appeals to you.

❖ If you like, you may figure out your "personality card" with the help of your birth date. You do this by adding the digits of your birthday. For instance, August 8, 1964, gives you: $8 + 8 + 1 + 9 + 6 + 4 = 36$. If the sum falls between one and twenty-two, the Major Arcana card with that number is your personality card. For instance, if the sum of the digits is nineteen, the personality card is "XIX–The Sun." If the sum is twenty-two, "XXII–The Fool" is the personality card.

❖ If the sum of the digits is twenty-three or higher, add the two digits of the number together to determine the personality card. For example, if the number is 36, the sum of the digits, $3 + 6$, equals 9, and your personality card is "IX–The Hermit."

RULES AND PRACTICE

You don't need a lot of instructions to work with Tarot. We've provided the rules that deal with the art of interpreting Tarot (starting on p. 49). The "correct" way to shuffle or to select cards, using either hand, and other similar "rules" are actually only customs rooted in fortune-telling. They are irrelevant for reading your own Tarot cards. The act of selecting a card can be as elaborate or as simple as you like. The magic of Tarot is in the symbols themselves and not in the external pattern.

Focus your attention on the card(s) you pull. You should be mentally, spiritually, and emotionally open-minded. Of course, you must have the courage to look the emotions and the realities that Tarot symbols represent squarely in the eye.

The easiest way to begin is with the card of the day. Pull one card daily, in the morning or in the evening. You'll use your card of the day as a symbol, a motivating force, or a reflection of the day.

Many people use a journal to keep track of the card of the day and the insights they have gleaned from it. Over time, such a journal can become a personal Tarot workbook and companion.

Our best advice is to find your own way, your own method, and stick with it. Separate yourself from preconceived notions and expectations, such as what is the "right" interpretation of a card. Generally speaking, preconditions and comparisons only hinder you from understanding the wonder of Tarot for yourself. And you'll only find the magic of Tarot when you experience for yourself the awe of the pictures and symbols.

RULES OF THE GAME

What you read into each card is most important. Allow the moment of recognition to settle in. Use the interpretations and impressions provided in the literature, but remember that your own perceptions are more significant.

- ◈ All seventy-eight cards have equal value. No card is inherently good or bad.

- ◈ Each figure, form, and color in a card (whether it is a man or woman, child or adult, human, or animal) can represent you or a part of you.

- ◈ Note the perspective from which you are viewing a card. Are you identifying with the figure in the card? If the card has more than one figure, do you see yourself in all of them? If not, which part do you think fits you? At the same time, each card might stand for people, things, or events in your environment. Thus, you must establish your relationship to the figures and the symbols in the cards.

- ◈ Each card has at least one positive and negative meaning. The deciding factor is what you experience and feel at the moment you reveal the face of the card. The personal, actual meaning of a card becomes specific in the communication between the card and the viewer.

- ◈ When you read the cards for yourself, direct your full attention to every individual card as you turn it over. At the same time, observe your own reactions and feelings. When you are fully involved in the process, concentrating on each card as you turn it over and observing with your inner eye your own reactions, you will have direct access to the cards as well as to your own experiences. You will then experience the "magic of the moment."

- ◈ Each card speaks for itself, but each card also carries different messages in different situations. Be open to the message.

Pick up the cards and hold them in your hand. Relax. Breathe deeply. Concentrate on the question your inner voice is asking.

WORKING WITH THE CARDS

Use all seventy-eight cards of your Tarot deck. The habit of using only the twenty-two cards of the Major Arcana stems from before 1910, when only the Major Arcana had pictures. Today, this practice does not make sense.

❖ Think of what question you want the Tarot cards to answer. You can ask any kind of question you want (see next page).

❖ Remember that the cards work like a mirror. Although you may ask questions about other people, the answers always take your relationship with those people into consideration. When you ask a question about someone else, remember that you are always an integral part of the "game."

❖ Shuffle the cards as you normally would. Any "requirements," such as pulling cards from the left, mixing and steering cards on the table surface, fanning cards in a circle, etc. are not necessary. We have nothing against personal rituals, but they are not rules.

❖ When reading your own Tarot cards, you should shuffle, lay out, describe, and interpret the cards yourself. If you are posing the questions, you should move the cards and have the first and final say in the interpretation. Anyone else present during a reading should be available for dialogue, company, support, and, if necessary, review and critique.

❖ Choose the layout beforehand. You may use the suggestions given in any Tarot book, or you may design one yourself.

❖ Select the cards in your usual way. Place them facedown in your chosen design.

- Turn the cards over one at a time. Wait until you have finished contemplating and interpreting one card before you turn over the next.

- Find the answer to your question in the complete layout of the cards.

WHAT QUESTIONS TO ASK

You can ask the Tarot cards any question that is important to you. What kind of question should you ask? Be guided by what is closest to your heart.

- In traditional fortune-telling, you should not read cards for yourself or a relative. Obviously, this rule does not apply to Tarot because that is exactly what we are doing—reading for ourselves and for others, regardless of what the relationship may be. On the other hand, we can't "read" for others. We can only show them how to do a reading for themselves.

- You may ask any question, including "Yes" and "No" questions. Depending on the situation, the answer may give you a certain direction or a certain connection.

- Because Tarot cards are like a mirror, the person doing the reading should always pull and interpret the cards. If several people are reading Tarot together, the person asking the question may or may not decide to tell the others what the question is. If the others know what the question is, they can refer to it as they interpret the cards. On the other hand, if they don't know the question, they can examine the cards and symbols intensely rather than merely exchanging assumptions.

- You'll find the answer to a question in the whole layout and not in any single card. When you have finished your interpretation, you may also want to determine the sum of the digits of all the cards in the layout. Add the numbers of all cards on the table (The Court Cards, such as the Kings and Queens and "0–The Fool" count as 0, and aces count as 1). You find the sum of the digits the same way as you found your personality card (see p. 25). The Major Arcana card corresponding to the sum of the number you have calculated is "the sum of the digits card," or "the Quintessential Card."

◆ The Quintessential Card represents a possible summary or headline for the layout. You can also use it as a control card for a cross-check. Remember, however, that the layout is complete by itself. The Quintessential Card adds nothing new.

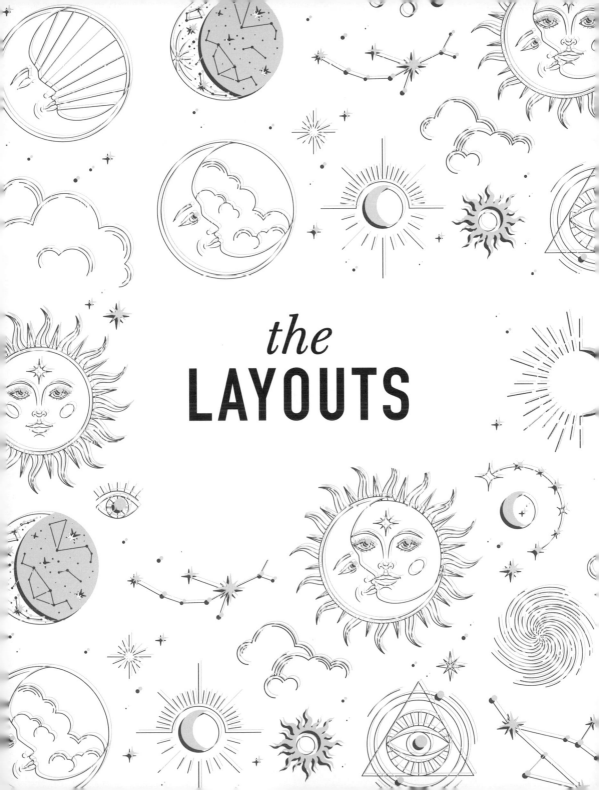

the LAYOUTS

TWO SPREADS FOR ALL EVENTS

1 Actual situation.

2 Past or how it began.

3 Future or what will be new for you.

1 Key or main aspect.

2 Past or how it began.

3 Future or what will be new for you.

4 Root or foundation.

5 Crown, chance, tendency.

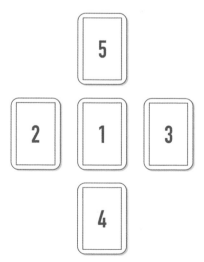

TENDENCIES AND PERSPECTIVES

1 & 2   Main message.

3   Root or foundation.

4   Heaven, chance, tendency.

1   The aspects that are already known.

2   The other side of the coin.

3   What needs to change.

4   The decision, the perspective.

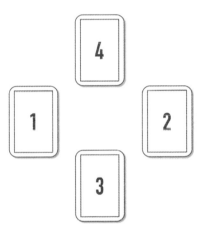

THE STAR

1   Where you are.

2   Your task.

3   Your difficulties.

4   Your strengths.

5   Your goal.

1   Where you are.

2   Your task.

3   Your fears.

4   The attitude that would be helpful.

5   The result of your efforts.

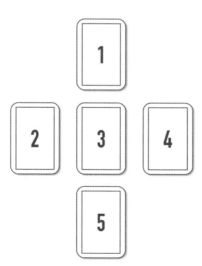

THE PENTAGRAM

1   This is where you came from.

2   This is where you are going.

3   This is what is difficult for you.

4   This is what makes sense.

5   This is your ultimate goal.

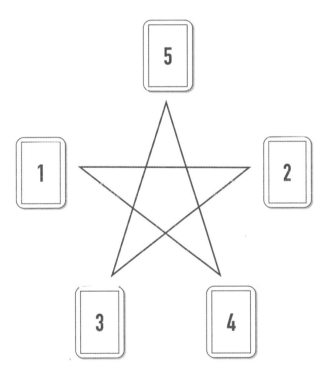

DECISION TIME

1 & 2 Where you came from.

3 & 4 Where you are headed, including the dangers/
chances.

1 & 3 This speaks against it.

2 & 4 This speaks in favor of it.

5 The decision.

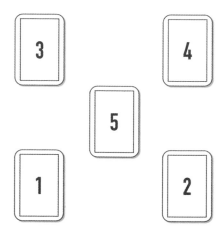

TAKING INVENTORY

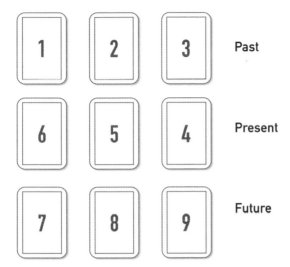

1   2   3   Past

6   5   4   Present

7   8   9   Future

THE SWORD

1 The heart of the matter.

2 Your starting point.

3 Your base or support.

4 Your chance/what will aid you.

5 A problem is being solved.

6 A desire is being fulfilled.

7 New knowledge, new insights.

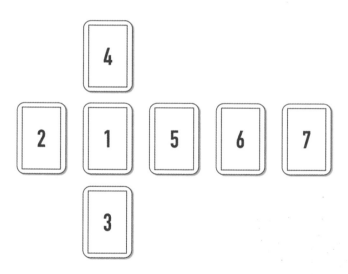

THE DREAM GOAL

1   Where you stand.

2   Where you are going.

3   Your aspirations.

4   Your fears.

5   Your true desire.

6   The secret of the search.

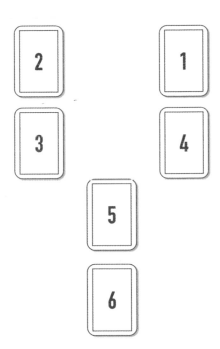

ULTIMATE HAPPINESS

1   This is what you will get rid of.

2   This is what you will achieve.

3   This goes with it.

4   What will bring you luck.

5   You will still be confronted with this.

6   The solution as a blessing.

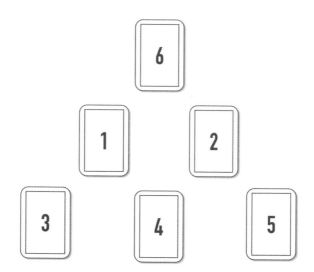

THE ROAD TO THE SOLUTION

1   Your dowry.

2   . . . its curse.

3   . . . its promise.

4   A challenge for you.

5   This will remain a puzzle to you.

6   This is a necessary burden for you.

7   Your task.

8   Your problem.

9   The solution.

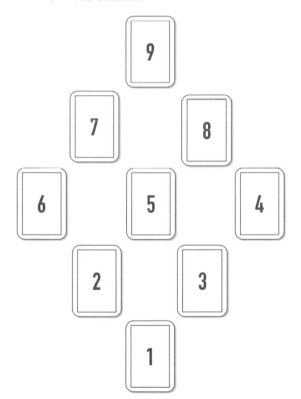

THE ROAD TO REACH YOUR DESIRE

These cards are chosen, not pulled, for this layout. The first card represents what is. Relax, concentrate, and choose a card that fits your present situation. Place it in front of you. Next, find a card for what should be, what you wish for. Take as much time as you need.

Once you have found and placed these two cards in front of you, spread them apart and find three more cards that serve as the connection or bridge to help you get from "what is" to your goal. Make sure that the three cards you pick for the bridge are able to "carry the weight" of getting you to the other side. In the end, look at the whole row as one path and one event (sum-of-the-digits number).

   1   **Present situation.**

   2   **What you desire.**

3, 4, & 5   **Bridge between Cards 1 and 2.**

FACING THE GAP

1   **This is possible.**

2   **This is important.**

3   **This is courageous.**

4   **This is futile.**

5   **This is necessary.**

6   **This is joyful.**

7   **This is funny.**

8   **This helps you get ahead.**

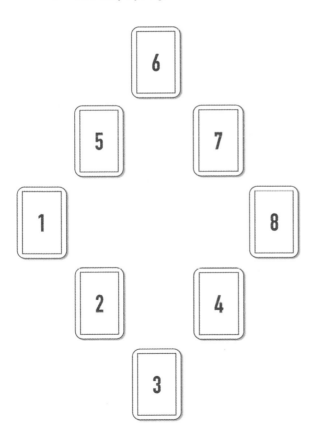

THE CELTIC OR SUN CROSS

 1 You and the argument in question.

 2 Positive addition to 1.

 3 Negative addition to 2.

 4 Root, basis, support.

 5 Crown, chance, tendency.

 6 The past or that which already exists.

 7 The future or what is new.

 8 Summary of positions 1–7; your inner strength, your subconscious.

 9 Your hopes and fears.

 10 Environmental and outside influences; your external face.

 11, 12, & 13 Summation, or a factor you are made specifically aware of because it is becoming increasingly more important.

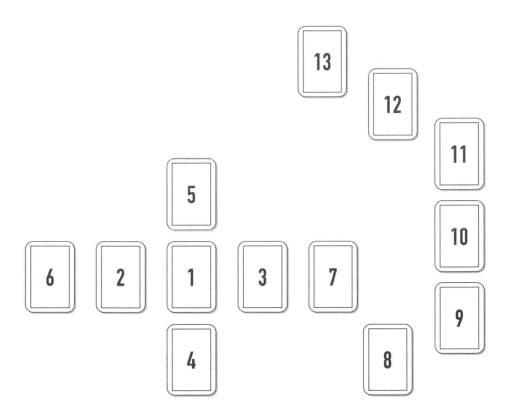

THE CELTIC OR SUN CROSS (VARIATION)

1   Starting point; theme of the question.

2   Cross card, opposing or complementary to 1.

3   Chances, culmination, conscious side.

4   Root, basis, unconscious side.

5   Past.

6   Future.

7   Inner strength, internal attitude.

8   Outside influences; the face you show the world.

9   Hopes and fears.

10   Outcome, goal, task.

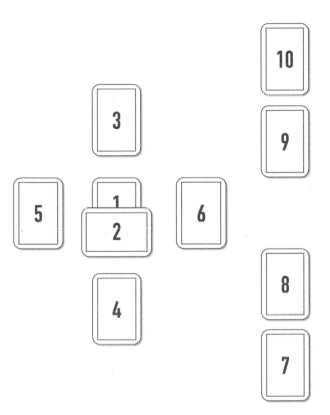

READING
for yourself

LEADING QUESTIONS

What do you see in this card?

❖ What does it remind you of? What events and images come to mind?

❖ What experiences have you already had with this card?

❖ What kind of experience do you connect with these individual symbols in the picture?

How do you see the picture?

❖ What type of images does this card remind you of?

❖ Specifically, what is it in the picture that speaks to you?

❖ With which of the figures in the card do you identify? From what perspective are you looking at the card?

What does this card mean to you?

❖ What is it that touches you?

❖ What kind of message are you receiving from this card?

❖ What connects you to this message?

How can you use this picture?

❖ What happens when you are involved with this card?

❖ Are you accepting the card's message?

❖ What is your next goal?

TOOLS FOR INTERPRETATION
STANDARD MEANINGS OF THE FOUR SUITS

WANDS

Wands represent fire. They stand for willpower, energy, zest for life, self-assertion, creativity, productivity, and growth. The world of the Wands involves intentions, actions, engagements, and realization of power. Wands deal with enterprise, arrival, identity, self-confidence, intuition, exuberance, and success. Aries, Leo, and Sagittarius are the astrological signs of the Wands and of the element of fire.

CUPS

Cups represent the element of water. They stand for the soul, the internal essence, and the unconscious. Their world is the world of feelings and premonitions, of the inner voice, and of spiritual experiences. They deal with inner perceptions and inner wisdom, with sense and meaning, joy, grief, emptiness, and fulfillment. Cancer, Scorpio, and Pisces are the astrological signs of the Cups and of the element of water.

SWORDS

Swords represent the element of air. They stand for the mind, mental energy, consciousness, reason, and the intellect. The world of Swords is the world of recognition, decision, ideas, and judgments. Swords deal with thoughts and concepts, with conscious and distinct perceptions of the world and oneself, with originality, freedom, the learning process, and clarity. Libra, Aquarius, and Gemini are the astrological signs of the Swords and of the element of air.

PENTACLES/DISKS

Pentacles/Disks represent the element of earth. They stand for the physical body, all kinds of matter, physical experiences, practical skills, applied talents, material creation, and for shaping the environment. Their world is the world of results, facts, products, physical awareness, and physical perception. They deal with work, nature, community, certainty, self-awareness, and being connected to the earth. Capricorn, Taurus, and Virgo are the astrological signs of the Pentacles/Disks and of the element of earth.

THE MINOR ARCANA

The following are standard suggestions for interpreting the individual stations of the Minor Arcana. When used with the information concerning the four suits presented above, the suggestions are a framework you can use with every one of the fifty-six cards of the Minor Arcana. Hopefully, they will stimulate you and help you check your own interpretation.

THE COURT CARDS

The Court Cards present the full potential of each respective element. By different characters they represent mature personalities.

QUEEN: Innovative, spontaneous, beginning.

KING/PRINCE: Thorough, well-founded, strengthening.

KNIGHT: Considering consequences, drawing conclusions, making changes.

PAGE/PRINCESS: Playful, probing.

SUGGESTIONS FOR THE STATIONS OF NUMBERED CARDS

1 (Ace) Origin and root. Both the goal and achievement. The characteristic power of the respective element. A curse and a blessing.

2 Consolidation or the breaking of the power of the elements. Differentiation, separation, unraveling; contrasting and complementary.

3 The "total subject" or the heart of the matter; basic problems or totality (synthesis) of the respective element.

4 Stabilizing, organizing, and completion. New challenges and validation.

5 Personal essence of the respective element. Versatility and concentration.

6 Decision, consolidation, changes. The whole as the result of transcending difficulty; the whole as an expression of complex contradiction.

7 "Sifting through," testing, sorting out, improving. Take a look at what is left in the sieve and what is not. Critical phase, puzzle, versatility, transformation, and completion in relation to the respective element.

8 Confrontation or harmony of strengths and weaknesses. Alternating blockage, balance, or support by different characteristics of the respective element.

9 Maturing, scrutinizing, becoming aware. Self-awareness, searching, and finding personal autonomy in dealing with the respective element.

10 Fulfillment, goal, starting point. Many "duties": the respective element provides strength for letting go and gaining.

THE MAJOR ARCANA

The cards of the Major Arcana represent individual and collective motifs.

With every card you may ask the following:

- ◈ In the past or traditionally, what was the meaning of the situation illustrated? (For instance, "V–The Hierophant": the pope or high priest.)

- ◈ What is the meaning of this traditional figure from the past today? (For instance, "V–The Hierophant": churches and other religious institutions losing meaning, search for personal guidance.)

- ◈ What does the figure illustrated mean to you? (For instance, "V–The Hierophant": the search for one's own "St. Peter," the rock in the storm, inner security; making yourself wholly independent "in heaven and on earth.")

THE SYMBOLIC MEANING OF THE COLORS

Here are some standard suggestions based on Western traditions. Of course, other cultures may know and apply quite different meanings for each color.

WHITE: Beginning (as an empty page) or fulfillment, integration, and healing. White shadow (animus). The harmonizing of spirit or new mental territory.

GRAY: Unconscious state or conscious equality; being unbiased.

BLACK: The unknown; the internal state of Earth or a fact; "black box," black shadow (anima), darkness of the soul or new spiritual territory.

RED: Heart, soul, will, vitality.

YELLOW: Sun, awareness, zest for life; envy, mental dissonance.

BLUE: Open sky or space and clear water; spirituality.

GREEN: Fresh, young, promising, inexperienced, immature.

BROWN: Connection between nature and earth; rooted, grounded, vegetative.

VIOLET: Experiencing boundaries; mixture of blue and red.

TEN GUIDELINES FOR INTERPRETATION

1. LEVELS OF MEANING

The process of interpreting Tarot cards takes place on several levels. The two most important are (1) the spontaneous and personal associations and (2) the guidelines of Tarot interpretation as developed over the last 200 years.

Most experts accept these guidelines. The most important is the allocation of the four antique Western elements—fire, water, air, and earth—to the four suits. If you don't know these traditional Tarot elements, you'll miss out on some very important meanings of the cards. Spontaneous and personal card associations, however, may express themselves on totally different levels from those of traditional guidelines. This is good because spontaneous associations express a very personal connection to a specific card, which is essential if you want to understand the practical aspect of the message contained in a card.

2. THE PERSPECTIVE OF INTERPRETATIONS

Interpreting Tarot cards is much like interpreting dreams: The interpretation of any card may refer to a subjective level and an objective level.

On the objective level, different figures in the card stand for people other than the viewer. In a sense, we encounter our colleagues, children, partners, friends, etc. when we look at the symbolic figures portrayed in Tarot cards.

On the subjective level, however, each figure is a mirror of the viewer's own self. Even if your partner, child, or colleague comes to mind when looking at an image, the figure associations and the figure are nothing more than a collection of symbols and aspects that are part of yourself.

3. SELF-AWARENESS

On a subjective level, all cards and details refer back to you. Therefore, it is important to observe yourself.

From time to time, you will come across the same card again and again. This is a card you should pay special attention to. In the course of observing yourself, you will notice that you react to some cards in the deck differently from how you do to others. You might be overjoyed when selecting these cards, or you might come across cards that leave you "cold." You may find that a specific card or the interpretation of a card is not helpful. You may even encounter a "stress card," a card that you instinctively reject and don't like to pull. Pay attention when this happens. Observe your emotions. These are cards and themes whose messages are not yet clear, and the fundamental rule is to make a mental note of the cards and the themes.

Also, keep track of particularly high and low points when interpreting the cards. This is important because we have difficulty with such cards and are unable to find an immediate solution.

Don't try to dismiss this. On the other hand, don't try to understand it immediately. Keep the subject matter in mind, just as you would make a note to remember items for your next trip to the grocery store. In this way, you "take" the unresolved matters with you into the day. Generally speaking, during the course of a few days or weeks, deliberate attentiveness produces the proper answer from within you.

4. PAST – PRESENT – FUTURE

Always use the present time frame when interpreting Tarot cards. The cards and symbols of Tarot are a mirror for what is.

However, we often recognize certain problems or dangers that stem from the past in the cards. Unusual, surprising, and curious images might be an indication of unknown possibilities that are already beginning to play into the reading of the Tarot cards.

5. ASSIGNMENT – CONFIRMATION

Each card may indicate that a task has been accomplished or has yet to be completed. The respective messages could be warnings, encouragements, or confirmations. If you are not quite sure which of the possibilities is the correct one at that moment, give equal weight to all of them. Remember to keep the different alternatives in mind (see Guideline 3).

6. THE DETAILS AND THE WHOLE

Many Tarot cards show details of symbols that are also a summary of the content of the whole picture. For instance, in the Waite-Smith card "IX–Pentacles," you will notice a snail in the foreground. The snail might imply a difficulty caused by facts that you fail to hide, but you leave the safety of your "shell." The same snail might also be a validation if it indicates that, no matter where you go, your house or shell is always with you, and you are at home no matter where you are. However, the snail also speaks of the whole card. The figure in the card might hide her splendor and radiance behind a tall hedge. On the other hand, the figure might represent a person who has found her proper place in the world and is at home with herself and the world.

In the Crowley-Harris "Princess of Cups," small crystals are visible at the edge of her gown. This detail reflects the content of the whole picture, including the notion that emotions have crystallized into specific wishes and passions. (That may encourage you to go for your desires, or it may warn you against a hardening or freezing of emotions.)

Be sure to pay attention to the details in a card and try to understand their importance in the context of the whole.

7. THE SHADOWS

Shadows are present even in pictures that are not particularly dark or black. Since ancient times, Tarot experts have used the shadow, or dark side, to represent that which is invisible or cannot be perceived. (The Greek god of the dark underworld is Hades, a word that literally means imperceptible.) You can interpret everything that is gray and undefined as the dark side.

The background is the classical example of shadow. The shadow follows our every step and remains unnoticed by us. In that sense, the back is another expression of "the blind spot." Cards that show the back of something (such as the figure in the Waite-Smith "III–Wands" and "V–Cups") give us a special insight because part of our task is to take a good look at the "other side of the coin," the dark side.

Cards in which everything is behind a figure remind us that we must take into account everything that is going on behind us. Such is the case with the Waite-Smith "IX–Cups" card. Although this card depicts nine cups, every cup is behind the figure in the picture. All feelings and emotions are in the background, hidden in the shadow. Only after you have had a conscious debate with "your cups" will the nine cups behind the figure mean that you have effective emotional and spiritual backing.

In cards dominated by black and darkness—for example, the Waite-Smith "IX–Swords" and "XV–The Devil"—the undefined shadow turns into blackness and darkness. All you have to do with these "black" cards is to make sure that you become aware of the unknown territory and distinguish between what this black unknown offers in positive terms and what is old baggage that you need to let go of.

8. A PICTURE WITHOUT A HUMAN FIGURE

Many Tarot decks have very few human figures in the Minor Arcana cards. Different versions illustrate the cards in different ways. For instance, in the Waite-Smith deck, almost every card has a human figure. In this deck, cards without a human figure are the exception. Thus, in the Waite-Smith deck, a card without a human figure is always a warning to the viewer not to lose sight of himself. In addition, such a card is also a kind of encouragement not to be bashful.

In the Crowley-Harris deck, as in other, older versions, only a small number of cards contain human figures. In this deck, almost all human figures appear as faceless objects. This could simply be an artistic treatment that creates a message by "covering" the mirror for the viewer. However, it could also be a warning that the viewer is "faceless" and needs to bring more of his or her own identity and personality into the deliberation.

9. PROPORTION

Take note of the proportion of the figures in a card. Proportions have particular significance in the Waite-Smith deck. For example, the small size of the figures in cards such as "IV of Wands" is significant. The card might depict a situation that keeps a person small and hinders growth. On the other hand, the size of the figure is fine and simply creates perspective to emphasize the relative height of the wands. This is a perfect example of how to create high tension.

10. REVEALING BEHAVIOR

When reading cards with other people, you may find yourself expressing ideas directly related to the interpretation of the image on a card, even if you didn't consciously mean to make such a remark. You may pull a particular card while talking with your friend about something seemingly unrelated, only to become suddenly aware that your conversation has added an entirely new interpretation to the card in front of you.

Everything that you say and do while you are working with a card can be part of the interpretation and message of the card. For instance, you might spontaneously straighten your body while uncovering a card. With a different card, you might bend over and feel slightly tired. The words that you utter as well as your body language might be interesting tips for the interpretation of a particular card.

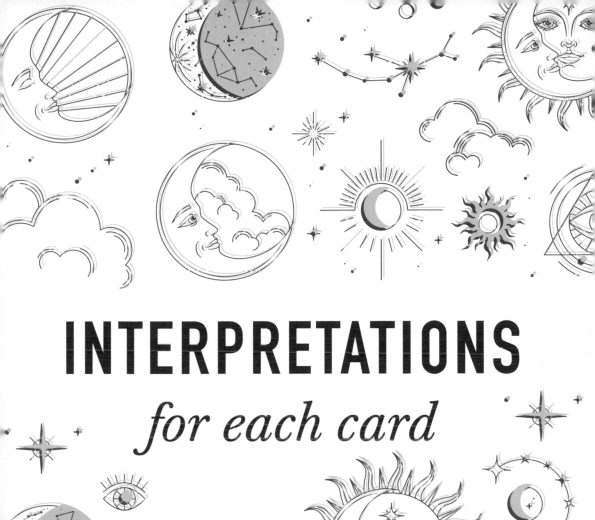

INTERPRETATIONS

for each card

THE MAJOR ARCANA

THE MAGICIAN.

THE HIGH PRIESTESS.

THE EMPRESS.

STRENGTH.

THE HERMIT.

WHEEL OF FORTUNE.

THE DEVIL.

THE TOWER.

THE STAR.

THE MOON.

THE EMPEROR.

THE HIEROPHANT.

THE LOVERS.

THE CHARIOT.

JUSTICE.

THE HANGED MAN.

DEATH.

TEMPERANCE.

THE SUN.

JUDGEMENT.

THE WORLD.

THE FOOL.

I.
THE MAGICIAN/THE MAGUS

HAS MAGIC ALREADY HAPPENED?

Magic does exist. You don't have to do anything; you don't need to perform any rituals. Magic is not fantasy or false promises. It is the power of individual self-fulfillment. We see this concept in the number "1," which is part of many numbers in Tarot. It is indivisible.

All the sensational images of magicians and witches as powerful heroes or villains that we see in films and read about in novels are totally without meaning. In the past, people believed that magicians possessed supernatural powers because they had mental and emotional energies that couldn't be explained any other way. What we need to do is discover the "magician" as a natural power available to all of us.

According to author Carlos Castaneda, "Every so often each one of us is given a cubic centimeter of a chance." Using that chance is what makes the difference.

Every one of us is given his or her own chance. When we experience our own "magic," we feel very alone, but that is the way each of us feels. Many individuals make a community.

You need imagination to answer personally relevant questions. Imagination is a gift that helps you find your own inner self. It is the spark that helps you recognize a void or find a bridge that is unique to your own situation. No one can give you your own "magical power," but no one can take it away from you, either. It will be visible to you alone.

*interpretations
for each card*

65

II.
THE HIGH PRIESTESS/
THE PRIESTESS

LUCK IS NOT A MATTER OF CHANCE

Actually, luck depends on fulfilling important wishes and releasing intrinsic fears. The first step is to recognize and name feelings, dreams, experiences, and expectations. The second step is to distinguish between those wishes that are useful to you and those that are not. Decide which of your fears are legitimate and which are not.

The language of our soul becomes clear only when we interpret it. Glorifying the power of the spirit indiscriminately is as frivolous and senseless as being indiscriminately skeptical about the psyche. Believing that dreams are illusions, that a display of feelings reveals weakness, and that intuitions are unreliable is as ridiculous as believing the other side of the coin, that you should only trust the power of the unconscious and that nothing more than your inner voice will show you the way. The motto for anything involving the senses and the heart should be first to define and then to connect.

The practical consequences of this card point in several directions. Sometimes, your task might be to create your own space and boundaries (a room of your own). At other times, your task might be to open the walls to the outside, blending your own feelings with those of others. You must first understand and then choose between what is spiritual and what is empty, what is blasphemous and what is faithful, and what is stimulating and what is simply shocking.

interpretations
for each card

67

III.
THE EMPRESS
WITH BODY AND SOUL

According to mythology, Venus, whose sign is part of the Waite-Smith and the Crowley-Harris cards, possesses a magic belt so alluring that she is irresistible. The emphasis on her waist should be seen in more than simply a sexual context. The waist is also a symbolic expression of the connection between consciousness and unconsciousness, between body and mind. The Waite-Smith card "III–The Empress" represents the union of heaven and earth, a crown of stars and material power. The Marseilles deck uses these same symbols. In the Crowley-Harris deck, the dark moons signify spiritual experience in its totality, the spheres of desire and reality, of freedom and necessity. These different "worlds" touch in the center of the card.

The essence of our being, our personal nature (which is always twofold) and human core, blossoms when we love and are loved. Humanity unfolds its creativity and truth when our sense and senses are given a chance.

Interestingly enough, Venus, the power of love, appears in the card independently by herself. That is not an accident. According to psychoanalyst Erich Fromm, when you cling to another person because you aren't able to stand on your own two feet, the other person might be saving your life, but the relationship is not love. Paradoxically, the ability to be alone is a prerequisite for loving.

*interpretations
for each card*

IV.
THE EMPEROR
PIONEER OF LOVE

When we understand that the "IV–The Emperor" is not the opposite of "III–The Empress" but rather a continuation, we understand why love also plays a central role in this card. Of course objections may arise. The title "The Emperor," with its picture of an armor made of iron, a throne made of stone (see Waite-Smith card), and other such motifs, conjures up images of the arrogance of power, stinginess, being closed up and hardened, and the male figure. But let us not forget that each card stands for both male and female. The point is how you "rule" and how you organize and motivate yourself.

The pictures also allude to the symbolic meaning of Aries. For the archetype of Aries, birth is more than a beginning. Birth is also a principle to live by. It is a call to start something, to do it, and to renew life. In the Crowley-Harris card, the Easter lamb indicates that life and not death is the most important element. Traditionally, people light a fire during Easter night to show their understanding of this concept. Another typical Easter motif involves changing a desert into a garden. In the Waite-Smith card, this symbolizes possibility and a task assigned while in the desert.

This card also refers to the power we possess within ourselves, the potential to discover, and the achievement of new possibilities in life and love.

interpretations
for each card

V.
THE HIEROPHANT

OPEN SESAME!

In many belief systems, the "V–The Hierophant," or high priest, had the ability to interpret the secrets of life and to organize the practice of rites and rituals. Today, the task is to discover, recognize, and use the power of "V–The Hierophant" in ourselves. We hold the key in our own hands!

This card shows how the large powers that we already have and the small powers dormant within us coexist and contradict each other. The interaction of all figures in the card is significant for its meaning of initiation and spiritual learning.

When you confront an actual situation and want to know how things are going to turn out, first ask yourself, "What is it that I've always wanted to know about myself that no one else can tell me?" This question is essential if you really want to integrate your personal strengths and weaknesses to get in touch with your quintessential self, which is implied in the Crowley-Harris card by the Pentagram (five-pointed star) and in other decks by the number V.

Pay attention to how you and others introduce and project yourselves. If what you say and how you present yourself are really an expression of what is inside you, then your essence and your appearance are in accord. This is how "Open Sesame!" works. When you pull this card, you only need to name and clearly demonstrate what is inside you and what you desire.

*interpretations
for each card*

VI.
THE LOVERS
LOVE AND COGNITION

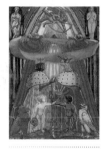

While we long for love, we might also be secretly afraid, afraid to be in love, or afraid of being loved. The ability to attain happiness with what we perceive as love depends on the goals and expectations that we connect with "love." The goals, motifs, ideals, and the guiding star of love are indicated by the spirits or angels that act on behalf of the spiritual perspective of the lovers.

As long as you are searching for your "better half," you are in danger of being only half a person. Additionally, when two "halves" come together, love is only a half-hearted affair. You also need to find out how relevant the concept of "love between equals" is for you. Are you still searching for someone just like you? If you are looking for a person with whom you are in total agreement, who understands you completely, you will find only one person—yourself.

The more pronounced the differences, the more fruitful the relationship! As soon as we are able to love the differences between us, a new paradise opens its doors! Love based on the individuality and uniqueness of two human beings finds fulfillment (depicted in the cards as an angel or spirit) in experiences that go way beyond what a single individual can attain. Therefore, the mandate here is twofold: praise the differences and reach for new heights.

interpretations
for each card

⋮

75

VII.
THE CHARIOT

DARE TO CHOOSE YOUR OWN COURSE

What is the most fateful relationship in life? The one we have with ourselves! The dynamic of the unconscious pulls us, drives us, stops us, and carries us.

We can't control and reign our karma, the unconscious, and our life histories, but we can try to find the proper inner attitude to these. As John Lennon said, your karma is going to catch up with you anyhow. Better to recognize who your brother is in everyone you meet.

The canopy of the wagon in the Crowley-Harris card bears the inscription, "ABRACADABRA." The unresolved contradictions in our lives give us the sense that something is "jinxed." To put it another way, when we deal with our inner impulses and our external goals and stop projecting, our magic reaches new levels. We need to protect ourselves from people who deny their own contradictions. We must have courage and vigorously challenge ourselves.

VIII/XI.
STRENGTH/ADJUSTMENT/
JUSTICE

CHOOSE THE FIGHT YOU FIGHT

The subject of inner attitude (see "VII–The Chariot") is not very far removed from that of justice. Justice is less a matter of abstract principles than of how we deal with right and wrong in our lives, how fairly we behave toward others, what course we choose to be honest to the multitude of desires, goals, needs, and expectations around us.

Ambivalent feelings and opinions about yourself and others go hand in hand with growing up. In order to be fair in your attitudes and your behavior, you must first examine your assumptions. You need to think about the obstacles and barriers in your way. For example, think about the uncertainty and difficulty you may have in identifying things and events, the difficulty you may experience in identifying where uncertain feelings come from, and your lack of knowledge of the meaning of certain perceptions. You must go through all of these again and again if you want to leave prejudice, egoistic fervor, and indifference behind.

The more careful your investigation, the more loving your judgments will be. You need the courage to criticize and to honor achievements when you ask timely questions, but nothing is as important as the willingness to be honest when deciding whom and what you really love.

*interpretations
for each card*

⋮

79

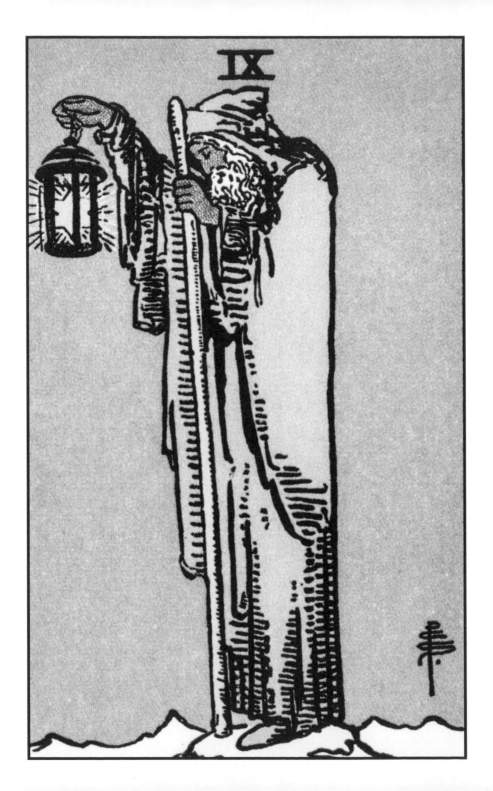

IX.
THE HERMIT

HEALING

The lantern of "IX–The Hermit" reminds us of the biblical parable of the wise and foolish virgins. (Wise virgins are attentive, with their lights always ready.)

Based on appearances alone, many people think "IX–The Hermit" symbolizes an old man, but he really symbolizes a virginal quality. Every human being brings something new to this world, something that never existed before and that would not exist without that person. (Compare the image of the universal egg and the sperm in the Crowley-Harris card.) When we overlook these images, we feel forsaken. However, when we understand our uniqueness, we can trust ourselves completely.

In addition, we need to use "light" to bring order into our world, to heal and bless it, to transform earth to a state of innocence. That is the meaning of the white earth underneath the figure in the Waite-Smith card. Cerberus, the three-headed dog in the Crowley-Harris card, suggests that the task is to remove the shadows from the past, the present, and the future.

The light encourages us to deal with the contradictions that surround us. We cannot understand the supreme power of "IX–The Hermit" by replacing irresponsibility with innocence or by retreating into dependency or incompetence. This figure represents the person who solves the problem and finishes the task without sweeping anything under the rug, regardless of what the task is.

X.
WHEEL OF FORTUNE
GREAT SOLUTION

The further you advance on the road of "IX–The Hermit," the more you understand that your good fortune lies in your fate. This means that you must use your talents for larger tasks, finding better solutions for shared problems that will expand and deepen your own awareness.

In a sense, this card is a warning not to adopt the attitude that you only want to endure long enough to get past a problem. That won't get you anywhere. Face up to your problems and find solutions. "Just getting through it" is a trap in which you can get lost.

The time is ripe for a new level of being and a larger frame of reference in which healing, wholeness, and regard for your own reality unite with your personal truth.

Stop cutting yourself up and stop cutting your life up into small chunks. Your love life, your work, your relationships, your thoughts, your energies, and all the different areas of your life are part of a whole. Find the thread woven through it! Summarize your experiences. Turn with all that you are, including your weaknesses and your strengths, to the tasks at hand.

XI/VIII.
JUSTICE/LUST/STRENGTH
GOING TO THE TOP

This card is a "hot" topic. *Hot* refers to the portrayal of sexuality that (in the Crowley-Harris card) is specific and obvious, or sexual. The same is true for the Marseilles and Waite-Smith cards, which show the head of a lion resting in a woman's lap.

Hot also means dealing consciously and willingly with the subject of sexuality. The Waite-Smith card uses blue mountains as a motif for the marriage of heaven and earth. The Crowley-Harris card shows the marriage of the visible or real world and the underworld.

We can think of the horizontal eight above the head of the woman in the Waite-Smith card and above the hat of the figure in the Marseilles card as signs of ultimate fulfillment. We can clearly see this is not merely a question of finding a high point here and there or of surviving a fleeting passion. We are dealing with deliberate contact with vital energy. This manifests itself in everything we utter.

Peak sexual moments have their own purpose. They give us a sense of energy, lust, and strength. In addition, they serve as examples of our ability to focus our personal energies and joys at any given moment on every aspect of our lives. Thus, we are to use all our energies and our personal talents living life to the fullest.

XII.
THE HANGED MAN
GREAT PASSION

At first, the figure in "XII–The Hanged Man" card looks somewhat disturbing. Surely, madness and absurdity are part of this card, but there is much more to it.

The card displays a definite point of view. The man's point of reference is not Earth, and he is not earthbound. He has a heavenly, transcendental perspective.

In one way or another, the man has reached the end of his rope. Whether it is a passion or patience, suffering for or loving somebody (or something), something has reached its highest level. When we learn to live life to the fullest, we can see this concept positively, living life at the greatest possible level of power and joy.

"XII–The Hanged Man" believes in what he is attached to, and he has firmly attached himself to that which he believes. It would be tragic if that belief turned out to be superstition. This card asks you to examine your own beliefs, to try to interpret the grounds for your feelings, dreams, and unconscious stirrings about all people. Once you are convinced that your belief system is valid, trust it completely. True convictions and a deliberate, clear passion are among the strongest emotions we can experience!

XIII.
DEATH
UNIQUENESS LIVED FULLY

This card stands for something that has come to an end. You will feel either sadness or joy, depending on whether it is something beautiful or awful. However, this card also says that there is something you have to finish. You are the reaper, and the sickle implies that you have the ability to make decisive changes.

The Crowley-Harris and Marseilles cards depict "XIII–Death" as the reaper, just as many fairy tales do. Sometimes we say that *death* means "letting go," but this interpretation is insufficient and one-sided by itself. The reaper is also a harvester who wants to bring home a harvest. That is his job. The Waite-Smith card implies this in the "Harvest Crown" flag he carries.

Let go in order to finish everything that is out of date, false, nonessential, and fruitless. Let go completely so that you may harvest that which is ripe and worthwhile.

If life is to be fruitful, you must do what is necessary to harvest what you want, including the big tasks that are the result of a lifetime of efforts. This harvest leads to a productive future. Which fruits are ripe now? Which results have yet to be achieved? What does not fit anymore? How can you accomplish what you wish for?

XIV.
TEMPERANCE/ART

TRUE WILL

The Latin verse behind the figure on the Crowley-Harris card reads: "*Visita Interiora Terrae Rectificando Invenies Occultum Lapidem,*" (the VITRIOL formula) or "Search for the inner region of the earth. If you do it right, you will find the hidden stone." The hidden stone refers to the "Stone of the Wise People," the center that alchemists tried to discover. But the stone of wisdom is the wisdom of the stone, which means that it resides in the earth, in matter. For that reason, you can remove, move, and change material contradiction.

    The great task and the goal of alchemy was to change "coarse" matter into "precious" matter and vice versa. Hundreds of years ago, alchemy stated a crucial point that was unheard of at the time but today is common knowledge: under certain circumstances, all solid matter expresses an equal value of a distinct quantum of energy.

    In practical terms, this card encourages you to take the contradictions of your life into your own hands. You should not ignore realities, nor should you capitulate to them. Realities are facts, and facts can be changed.

    Fire is a cleansing process that removes and burns waste products, allowing true intentions to appear and grow strong. The gaps between desire and reality, between the conscious and unconscious will, can be bridged. Relish the change in which previous facts are molded into something new.

*interpretations
for each card*

      ⋮

91

XV.
THE DEVIL
QUESTIONING VALUES

Every human being brings something unique into this world, something that did not exist before and would never exist without the person (see "IX–The Hermit"). Every human has a gift within him- or herself. But every one of us also brings characteristics and qualities that do not necessarily fit into the framework of established norms. These are gifts that remain in the dark, where they are ignored, considered taboo. As soon as "XV–The Devil" shows his face, this taboo is violated. What was hidden before is now visible. This is what makes "XV–The Devil" so special. We only need to know how to take advantage of him.

Don't be upset. You have a chance to sow some wild oats. On the one hand, "XV–The Devil" represents an old-style "vampire," a heavy burden that has made your own life and that of others quite difficult. You have a right to be afraid of him, but you can now shed this part of your shadow because you realize his true nature and how the respective inner part of you is acting. On the other hand, "XV–The Devil" represents a kind of orphan within you. That is an inner part of you that you have paid little attention to in spite of the fact that you secretly long to acknowledge it. Now you can claim the orphan. Whenever you bring light into darkness, the vampire disintegrates into dust, and the former orphan gains form and strength. Face the unknown and study it until you know what is useful for you and what is not.

XVI.
THE TOWER
COURAGE IN DIRECT ENCOUNTERS

This card represents two distinct archetypes: the tower of Babel and the events of Pentecost. The tower represents the specific male capacity to use force and to indulge in delusions of grandeur. These traits are responsible for the destruction of the tower and the loss of language. As a result, people no longer understand each other. The white dove with the palm leaf in Crowley-Harris and the golden tongues of flames in Waite-Smith are reminiscent of Pentecost, which is the exact opposite of the tower of Babel. The Holy Ghost appears to the disciples as tongues of flames. The disciples begin to speak, and people hear the spoken words in their own language. The limitations of speech and understanding are removed.

The tower of Babel and Pentecost, two opposite poles, present us with the opportunity to use the most powerful energies: violence and love. They are also two entirely different ways of going overboard. Using destructive force leads to speechlessness and confusion. Using love removes language barriers and allows communication and understanding to flow across all boundaries.

This card has no middle of the road. A crisis might be near, but you are dealing with a process which allows you to relinquish your mask and your reservations, your tower of Babel. Use all of your energies! The more deliberately you use these powerful energies, the better you protect yourself from forceful, unreasonable demands. Risk being more direct.

XVII.
THE STAR

DISCOVER THE STAR YOU ARE

How can a person be enlightened if he or she does not have a light within him? In order for your light to shine, all you need to do is to bring it out. This means that you must let go of all false inhibitions and reservations and open yourself to your own truth. And when this light shines at night and brightens your days, your wisdom will show itself in all its splendor. Sometimes, however, this card warns you against brazenness. The foot of the woman on the water in the Waite-Smith card represents two completely opposite psychological interpretations. Water symbolizes the soul, and in one interpretation, the soul is strong and capable of carrying the load. The water literally lifts you up from the unconscious. In the other interpretation, this is a warning sign that the soul is shutting itself off, feeling inadequate, and turning to ice. These are the dangers facing a person suffering from narcissistic self-love or a long-lost love for a distant "star."

In other words, allow your frozen feelings to melt. Keep the life of your soul flowing and work with your dreams and visions. You can dispose of hopes and fears, as the two pitchers that the woman is holding in her hands demonstrate. Creative dreams want to be realized and frightful dreams need to be dealt with. Neither can be accomplished in dreams, only through the conscious attention that flows effortlessly throughout your whole being.

interpretations for each card

XVIII.
THE MOON

REDEMPTION

"XVIII–The Moon" stands for great dreams, ancient, collective beliefs, and "oceanic" feelings. Like the image of the crayfish in the Waite-Smith and Marseilles cards and of the scarab beetle pushing the sun up from a great depth in the Crowley-Harris card, "XVIII–The Moon" brings hidden, primeval feelings and omens to light. The card shows heaven alive and churning, the journey of life, Providence, and many other layers of energy. Just as on a night with a full moon, emotions are easily stirred. Here, you are asked to confront some of your most overwhelming feelings.

Maybe you are dealing with mood swings right now, but you can't easily identify them. The danger lies in letting yourself be absorbed by the emotional roller coaster. Instead of merely stepping into the picture, you might consider diving into it, like the crayfish or the scarab beetle, and howl at the moon like the dogs. Of course, you can also choose to just stand there and be petrified, like the towers.

Your big advantage now is your ability to put yourself in the shoes of every living being. Nothing that is human is foreign to you, and you will be equally at home in the past, present, and future. You will learn to move and stand securely on your own two feet. You will acquire an expanded ability to recognize what is godly and what is private in each human being and in every event. This is a card that encourages you to open your heart and let go of apprehension.

*interpretations
for each card*

⋮

XIX.
THE SUN

ZEST FOR LIFE

From a human perspective, "XIX–The Sun" presents the new day as it comes up over the horizon. And so it is with this card, which represents actual and constant birth. It carries new life. For an adult to be like a child again, he or she must live from the center.

The term *midlife* refers to more than a person's age. It also refers to the person's energy. Depending on their state of consciousness, it is possible to grow again, and to experience vitality at any time. This kind of life energy is independent of a person's age. However, as soon as we have outgrown childhood and adolescence, it takes a conscious act in order to be a child again. This means a personal dedication to "life's longing for itself," as Khalil Gibran put it. The French scholar Henri Bergson named it the "élan vital"—the implicit intention to live and to grow.

When dedicated to this way of living, we replace conventional behavior and thought with a lifestyle we choose deliberately as the correct one for us. We select our relationships independent of our blood connections (of course, we may choose relatives too). We make decisions about large and small events based on our will and by conscious choices instead of living by the dictates of habit and repetition. Becoming and remaining a grown-up child is the way to stay in the zest, the flowing energy of life, open to all beings.

*interpretations
for each card*

⋮

XX.
JUDGEMENT/THE AEON
A REAL TRANSFORMATION

Traditionally, the Marseilles card reminds us of the Christian message of the Last Judgment. The Crowley-Harris card seems to represent a turning away from the traditional image. Its title, "The Aeon," means a new era or a new calendar. The content of the Crowley-Harris card, however, remains true to the traditional meaning. It depicts the process of birth, adding the themes of revelation, transformation, and resurrection.

Everything is put on the table here, including relationships, problems, and new possibilities that you have been "pregnant" with for a long time. Until now, these are areas that you have been avoiding. This card is also an invitation to look at the extremes in your life, to analyze them, and to connect them. Basic desires and fears, feelings of guilt and self-recrimination must be dealt with again and again until all of the past and the horizon of the future are clear and clean. Only then will change mean that you are discovering and establishing new qualities in your life, that you have transformed what was old. Without remembering, repeating, and working through (as Freud would say), a rebirth would only mean repetition (think of the movie *Groundhog Day*); then today is already old when the sun comes over the horizon because it is just like yesterday.

Spread your arms, make peace, or say good-bye. Learn to forgive without forgetting. Draw a line under that which was.

XXI.
THE WORLD/THE UNIVERSE
RESOLVING CONTRADICTIONS

As far as its numerical value is concerned, this card is the
highest of the twenty-two "Great Secrets" of Tarot. What
would be more natural than to assume that this card means
award, victory, and culmination because it is at the end of the
journey through all the other stations? Such an interpretation
might be logical, but it is actually superficial. In the first place,
this assumption is based on wishful thinking: "All's well that
ends well."

The crown of laurels represents the crown of death
as well as the crown of victory. The horizontal eight that is
present in all three card versions is a symbol of infinity and
of the promise of harmony and balance. Nevertheless, it can
also mean the eternal repetition of the same thing and, in that
sense, it might also represent a vicious circle. This card is a
signal that you might be going around in circles because you
are so captivated by a subject or situation that you need to
distance yourself from it.

Alternatives are always available. That is the meaning of
the two magic wands held by the "world woman." Nothing can
be understood in and of itself. Every subject has a counterpart.
Your task now is to step into the center. The goal of dealing
with the polarities of life is to discover your personal values
and to determine what is truly essential for you in this world.

Link your present questions and concerns to your life's
goals. What contribution can you make to the world, or what
part can you play, that will require and activate the most of
your talents and potential?

*interpretations
for each card*

⋮

105

0.
THE FOOL

ZERO AS MODEL

This is the beginning and the end of that which makes you a
unique person. You can and must have the courage to face the
future, even if you cannot predict or determine the future in
advance. You must have the courage to walk your own path
and to be open, even if your back isn't covered, and even if conventional wisdom and common sense suggest otherwise.

The more independent the road you are traveling, the
greater the panic that may set in. In Greek, the word for *everything* is *pan*. So, *panic* means, "everything at once." The more
room "0–The Fool" has to move in your life, the more you
will get used to letting God, the world, and yourself be what
they are. Everything that you know and understand will take
its proper place in your life, and everything will occur at the
right time.

Look for the feeling that you are missing something
important, something meaningful. That will give valuable
hints. "0–The Fool" means that you are happy, without any
desire or anxiety. There are two quite different ways to meet
this state of "nothing left to lose." One way is to quit and
dismiss all wishes, needs, and longings, leaving nothing to
lose, as we've already lost it all (or never had it). "0–The Fool"
is warning against this. The other is to fulfill our important
desires and resolve our urgent fears. In doing so, we have
nothing left to lose as we have all that is meaningful in us.
Nothing can prevent us from being a part of all that flows on
within and without us. We realize our share of eternity. For
this, "0–The Fool" is encouraging us.

*interpretations
for each card*

107

Vitality and Heart · Willpower · Élan vital · Intentions · Intuition

WANDS THE MINOR ARCANA

WANDS REPRESENT FIRE. Their key element is willpower. Just as fire purifies a precious metal by burning and eliminating impurities, so does the fire of life purify the will.

The flames are constantly in motion when wood burns, and when you are in motion, you show the "fire" within you. The first meaning of a Wands card is that something needs to be done. You are looking for something, and the answer is at hand if you set yourself and others in motion or if you allow yourself to be set in motion.

The significance of motion is immediately recognizable when looking at the Wands card in the Crowley-Harris deck. Lightning-quick flames are leaping upward, expressing the dynamics of fire. In the Waite-Smith deck, Wands cards display green sprouts at the top of each wand. They clearly point to the main themes of fire: energy and acceleration. The sprouting also stands for the personal drive that is inherent in all of us. Even when the wands are bare wood without anything green, as in the Marseilles deck and older variations, they symbolize germination and growth because they are fuel, potential energy, and nourishment for the fire.

Other associations concerning Wands include wood that feeds the fire, the phallic symbol, a witch's broom, offspring or children, roots or ancestors, vitality, the use of energy, fireworks, hellfire, male inheritance, the sun, and the concept of "knock on wood."

*interpretations
for each card*

⋮

109

QUEEN OF WANDS

STAMINA

According to conventional wisdom, the "Queen of Wands" represents the heart of the fire. She represents your basic instincts.

Her particular strength and task are to provide the initial impetus. Think of the eventual consequences of your actions, but concentrate on what it is that will get you moving and on how to go about doing it. The strength of your self-esteem and a lively sexuality guarantee your success and well-being.

Understand that your directness, spontaneity, and independence are very special talents that others admire or acknowledge as long as you accept that others may be completely different. Don't fall into the trap of becoming impatient. Simply walk your own path. You can overcome the fear of flying, the fear of finding real peace, and other natural fears if you let the sunshine in your heart. Approach your tasks as steps and take every one of them with assurance.

KING/PRINCE OF WANDS

TEST BY FIRE

You are "hot stuff," active with a passionate heart and a spring in your step. Your actions are vibrant and lively as indicated by the green shoes and background. In the Waite-Smith deck, the throne has no defining top. This symbolizes that the sky is the limit.

The salamander (shown in the Waite-Smith card) is supposed to be able to walk through fire without being destroyed by it. If you walk the road of the salamander, you can connect heaven and earth, connect your will with what is necessary. You, too, will survive the test of fire. You need the fire because only fire separates gold from its impurities, and only fire can combine all your energies into one wish.

If you have a positive attitude toward the "test by fire," you will find it much easier to distinguish healthy from unhealthy stress. Healthy stress compels you to find and remain in your center, preventing you from idling and becoming distracted. Take advantage of this special chance or situation that presents itself. Take action. Don't start pulling back. This is a crucial moment. Confront stubbornness and heroics with actions that you wholeheartedly enjoy—for which you would walk through fire. Just do it.

KNIGHT OF WANDS
SHOW YOUR COLORS

As a knight, you are living in the middle of the fire. In order not to burn yourself, you must rely on your good sense and your intuitive ability to react. You won't be able to avoid the horse, which stands for vitality, a natural instinct, and drive. Your motto here is: "How can I find out what I want even before I am aware of what I am doing?"

Come out of your shell and express your inner thoughts, not without considering eventual losses, but without any expectations. You must act before you know the why. Keep moving because only action brings you closer to your goal. Meanings and events will become clear as soon as things begin to happen.

Put your energy to good use. Trust your intuitions and follow them. Unused energies turn into dead weight that only tires you and makes things more difficult. The fire uses and renews every ounce of energy that you can bring to the task. React to impulses and developments in your environment. Make sure that your goals and your life's tasks are big enough and worthy of the energy you bring to them.

*interpretations
for each card*

115

PAGE/PRINCESS OF WANDS

FIRE AND FLAMES

The Page/Princess lives where the drive is larger than life's experiences. The thirst for action and the yearning for progress has put you squarely in front of the task so that you can grow beyond your limits.

When comparing what you want to "move" and what is "moving" you, your experiences are relatively unimportant. Therein lies the danger and your chance. Don't get lost in the wasteland, and don't miss your chance. Now is the time for a new beginning that will lead you to the point at which you will discover the energy of your fire.

Just as you once came into this world filled with the will to live, with an innate desire for growth, and with natural drives, now you must rediscover life, playfully conquering and greeting every success and every failure, every event and every new experience with enthusiasm and abandon. As author Hermann Hesse said, "In each beginning is a magic that protects us and helps us to live."

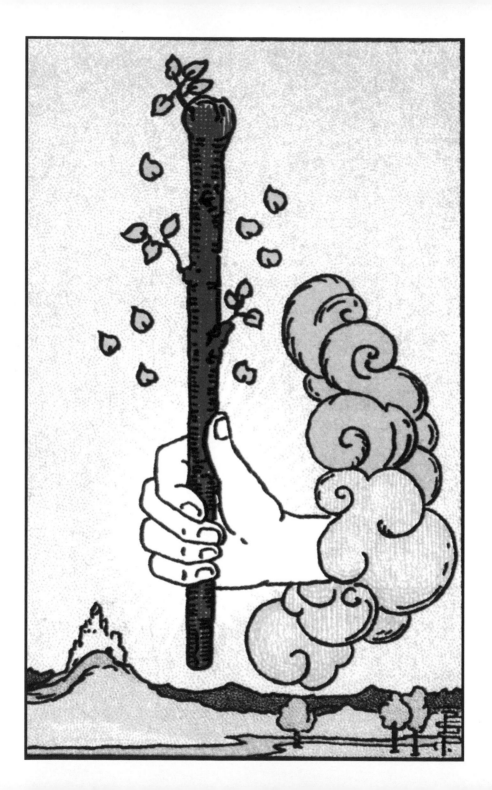

ACE OF WANDS

VITALITY

Without fire, you'll miss the flame of enthusiasm, the color of being alive, and the dynamics of desire. The most wonderful accomplishments do not bring happiness or lasting satisfaction if we cannot find a "wand" to convert our desires, intuitions, and pronouncements into deeds.

Surprisingly, we renew the energies of the fire inside us by using them. Some past experiences might keep us away from the fire: "Once burned, twice shy." But it is exactly because of such injuries that we now must master the fire.

Your contribution should be to change indifference and to halt the violent powers of fire in the world.

The hand reaching out from the cloud in some card designs means that life has given you the chance to detect the fire anew and is asking you to take it in your hand. The will to live and the joy to grow beyond your limitations are the two opposite poles of the fire wand. Embrace them.

II OF WANDS

TRUST IN YOUR OWN POWER

Without the joy and burden of beginning, you must divide a large task into smaller, manageable parts! "Divide and conquer" is the motto. You must divide your fire, contradictory motifs and goals, powerful instincts, and immediate and long-term tasks so that you can handle them successfully.

If you detest the arrogance of power, you are not allowed to faint. Distinguish between your own intentions and those of others, and work step-by-step with your own intentions and the energies of others.

Don't be caught in a catch-22. No one is forcing you to burn yourself out. You don't have to follow someone else's golden rule. The ball is in your court. Wait until you have a clear picture, until you have decided what to do; but when you are ready, don't hesitate. Play ball! Act with all of your might.

III OF WANDS

WITH ENTHUSIASM

Although we have many reasons for doing so, we often live with decisions that are bad choices. Some people are adventurers who "live with their fire" and are at home anywhere and nowhere. On the other hand, some people want the comfort of their own home where they can "rest," where the fire is only a pilot light. Lustful sexuality and tender love are often perceived as irreconcilable contradictions. Sometimes we hate the stress and the routine of work so much that we only feel like real human beings when we are on vacation or away from the office. And sometimes we don't seem to know what to do when not at work because only work seems to bring success and happiness.

We can't always avoid the contradictions of life, and we can't always resolve them. But all are poor choices and signs of crisis because they always cut us into pieces. However, a crisis is often the mother of invention. Thus, among other things, the Crowley-Harris card "Virtue" implies that your fire, your thirst for action, and your ingenuity are most effective when making a virtue out of necessity.

When you focus your undivided attention and all of your energies, you will find better solutions. The mindful implementation of your intention will bring you to your goal. Put your heart to it and act.

interpretations
for each card

123

IV OF WANDS

THE EYE OF THE TIGER

When you place power and spirituality, vitality and light in
a circle facing each other, like the ram and the dove in the
Crowley-Harris card, you are looking into the eye of the tiger,
the center of fire. The Waite-Smith card, too, shows life as a
powerful center accompanied by high tension.

The Crowley-Harris card uses the images of Venus and
Aries. The equivalent in the Waite-Smith card is the blue and
red color of the figures in the center of the card. We think of
Venus as typically female and Aries as typically male. Recognizing both the male and female genders is your essential
source of power. In addition, the relationship between Venus
and Aries urges you to discover the strengths and weaknesses
of the other gender in yourself as another challenge and
source of power.

If you are able to live with all the contradictions and
energies that are part of you and that stand between you and
the people in your life, you will always need and create new
determination and enthusiasm. Do not be frightened by the
challenge of the moment that seems contradictory. Avoid unhealthy stress as well as idle time. Consciously engage in your
relationships and the tasks at hand. In this way, all your energies will have a chance to become involved. Find the courage
to overcome limitations and contradictions so that you can
discover new creative possibilities in them.

*interpretations
for each card*

V OF WANDS

LIVING WILLPOWER

What you really want is not simply intrinsic; your will is actually in constant motion. It is truly to your advantage that your desires and interests compete with each other about what needs to be satisfied first. In the Waite-Smith card, this is symbolized by the fray. Here's a good example of what happens. On the one hand, a voice says, "I really want to get a good night's sleep." On the other hand, a voice says, "It's high time for me to go out and party." You have the household chores to do and the children to take care of, but there is the wanderer in you. You have passions and a need for approval, the desire for success, and much, much more.

Only when many "fires" are burning can your personal will remain alive and renewed, as emphasized in the Waite-Smith card. At any moment, the many forces involved could come together so that the energies do not dissipate. In the Crowley-Harris card, the wand placed prominently in the foreground depicts this aspect. The end result is that your energies gain vitality and clarity. At the same time, you preserve your playfulness because you did let go of fierce determination or indecisiveness.

Watch yourself and others. Test which part of your will pushes authentic desires and is able to put things in motion. What willful tactics are frivolous and used simply because you want to force something that has no merit?

VI OF WANDS

TOTAL INVOLVEMENT

Your optimal energies will unfold if you use both your strengths and your weaknesses. Indeed, you can make use of your weaknesses. It is not true that you can only succeed if you present your sunny side. If you allow yourself your weaknesses, you will be fully engaged and feel good about yourself. In this context, you have already won, no matter what you do. Otherwise, your victories will only be half victories, because you have sacrificed your right to be a whole person.

The more clearly you can identify with the hero and with all the other figures in the Waite-Smith picture, the more diverse, well-organized, and stimulating your fire will be. It will grow and influence others (note the images of the Crowley-Harris card). You can even change weaknesses into strengths. Those who ignore their weaknesses lose support, steadfastness, self-respect, and much more. If you change weaknesses into strengths, you will gain energy with every step you take.

Don't let others discourage you and don't hide your light! Trust that which you know to be your truth and stand by it. Then you will be like a runaway fire; nothing can stop you!

VII OF WANDS

ENERGY WORK

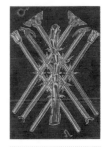

You have many different energies at your disposal. Your job in this card is to use them and sharpen them. You must put everything, all your intentions and goals, in one basket. For that reason, avoid casual decisions made without passion. If you want to achieve something, you must get in touch with it. If you want to move something, you must take it into your hands. If you want to change something, you must try to understand it. The more clearly you face reality, the greater the chance that your willpower will prevail. Any attempt to use manipulation in order to force your will on others becomes superfluous or even a hindrance.

Take your will and use it like a measuring tape, allowing the tape to change and be redrawn. When you actively work with your will and with the reality that confronts you, you will gain an invaluable advantage because you will know that desire and reality are no longer unbridgeable contradictions.

Be willing to be open in order for you and your environment to grow, change, and develop. You can change existing facts. The way things are evolving gives you new arguments and different powers in order to stand up for those things that are close to your heart. You will make a new beginning and raise your efforts to a new level.

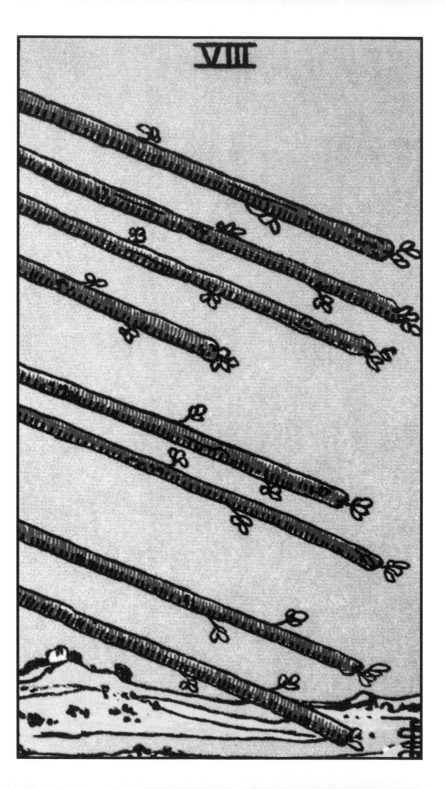

VIII OF WANDS
GREATER RESPONSIBILITIES

You are experiencing and making changes on many levels. Speed is no longer synonymous with magic. Your energy increases, making many more things possible than you ever imagined.

Many projects fail, not because you lack the courage to try something new, but because you lack the resolve to say good-bye to the old. Precious habits and old perceptions can be like a wall, preventing you from seeing the world as it really is, as in the Waite-Smith card. If you are guided by what you really want, you are free from obstructions and inhibitions without harm or unwanted loss.

As you proceed on this new level, you will have experiences and encounters that you would not have thought possible before. You will widen your horizon and expand your personal frame of reference, achieving new perspectives and insights. Your ability to assimilate these new awarenesses and to work with them is now possible and will be the secret of your success. Be open to new experiences, even to new realities. Do not lose sight of your goal. Don't let anything stop you or ruffle you. Demand the same determination from all the people around you. React with flexibility to demands and objections. You possess and need a greater measure of responsibility in areas that you are really concerned about.

IX OF WANDS

FULL ATTENTION

When the sun and the moon pull in the same direction (see Crowley-Harris card), our conscious wishes, represented by the sun, and our subconscious wishes, represented by the moon, are in alignment. It is as if big brother and little sister are walking hand in hand.

Whenever the sun and the moon are exactly opposite each other, we have a full moon. As long as we are in daylight, we are not aware of the full moon. This might be the case with the human figure in the Waite-Smith card. Many things are happening and many things are moving and developing, but all of this is behind his back, where most of the wands are. However, as soon as it is night, we become aware of the full moon. When we finally know consciously what our subconscious is trying to tell us, we might become agitated. This often happens at the full moon. Indeed, the more wands that were hidden from our view, the greater the uncertainty, the excitement, and the wonderment about all that finally comes to light during the full moon.

The bandaged head of the figure in the Waite-Smith card may indicate that a one-sided orientation of the conscious might cause you injury. The same bandage might be a sign that the figure is a fighter on his journey and represents the new awareness with which you are experiencing your days and nights, a new understanding of your complex needs. Take yourself by the hand and be your own big brother and little sister.

*interpretations
for each card*

X OF WANDS

TOTALLY FOCUSED

In the truest sense of the word, the X of Wands in the Waite-Smith deck shows heightened energy! To be precise, the Waite-Smith card shows two bundles of energy: the wands gathered in the middle and the figure carrying the bundle forward. The figure requires a "bundle of energy" so that he can follow his desire and/or master a task. The prominent display of two wands in both the Crowley-Harris and Marseilles cards creates the image of two great powers confronting or accompanying each other.

All of us possess our own logic, our own "law," and our own will. Success or failure depends entirely on how our own will and that of another are in harmony or discord.

If you feel that you have too much on your plate or are stuck on a one-way street, your will is in conflict with the will of another person or another reality. Find out where your will-power is weak and give 100 percent. However, if you find out that you are trying to get your way by force and self-denial, give up those futile efforts, let go, and unload the burden!

Only after you have given a person or a subject your undivided attention will you understand the logic involved. You must bend, venture forward, immerse yourself. Always look forward.

Soul · Feelings · Emotions · Desires · Faith · Spirit

CUPS REPRESENT THE ELEMENT of water. The key concept is the soul. Whenever you pull a Cups card, the first practical meaning is to make sure that your soul flows. Your soul will show the right answer or the right solution. Stay in tune and keep everything flowing. Bear in mind the needs of others and take into account all valid feelings.

You cannot grasp water literally or figuratively. A cup makes it possible to capture water. As water symbolizes our feeling, cups represent that which gives form to the otherwise unfathomable power of our souls. In Tarot, Cups represent the epitome of our feelings. But most of all, they represent our desires and fears; they help make the "flowing" needs of our soul fixed or concrete.

Other associations with Cups include the female womb and female estate, the knight's search for the Holy Grail, the source, the mouth or destination, the water of life and death, the fountain of youth, baptism, tears, drunkenness, and the moon. About three-fourths of Earth and two-thirds of the human body consist of water.

*interpretations
for each card*

139

QUEEN OF CUPS

WORTH OF THE SOUL

When we are confronted with the wealth of our feelings, we often believe we have too many feelings or that they are too enmeshed or too changeable, that they prevent us from having good relationships with ourselves or others. Generally speaking, that is not the case. In truth, only when we allow our feelings to flow freely can we clearly define the natural boundaries of our intuitive abilities. These are the boundaries that tell us that we have reached the limits of our capacity, which distinguishes our spirit from that of other people. At that moment, the cup is covered (see Waite-Smith card), and we become capable of having relationships in which being connected and alone, sharing a home and living by ourselves, and having compassion and self-awareness can live successfully side by side.

The need for spiritual wholeness presents a rather interesting contradiction. The Waite-Smith card depicts the soul as being both open and self-contained. The shell or funnel-shaped back of the throne is open, but the cup is covered with a lid. The Crowley-Harris card illustrates the same principle in a different form. Here, the soul is like a large mirror that is open to everything on one side yet closed and contained on the other side. The opposite poles of being open and protecting your privacy are essential for a sound spiritual life. Make sure you are open spiritually and protective of your own soul at the same time. When you do that, your feelings will be correct. You will speak as one person, with one voice.

KING/PRINCE OF CUPS
SUSTAINING DESIRE

Like the "King/Prince of Cups," you will feel adrift as long as you are looking for security from without. But the reverse is also true. You will find strength and inspiration when you are sure of your inner desires and hold on to the things that stimulate you. As soon as you are clear about your inner feelings, you will have a base of authentic feelings on which you may safely build (like the fish in the Waite-Smith card).

Strangely enough, it is your desire that gives you a sense of security, even though you find yourself in an ocean without a shore. This desire distinguishes itself from mere feelings by the heightened sense of awe and obligation it produces. Intense longing and passionate desire intensify your feelings, providing the foundation for your behavior. Try to get to the bottom of the present questions and to the feelings of all involved. Pay attention to deep-seated needs and have the courage to find your true desire and to express it.

KNIGHT OF CUPS
WINGS FOR THE SOUL

When feelings, spiritual needs, and spiritual desires take on extraordinary powers, it is impossible to confirm or disprove them on the basis of previous experiences. Powerful feelings are always a matter of belief, too. Sensible or conscious beliefs go hand in hand with knowledge and awareness. Beliefs and faith begin where reason and knowledge reach their very limits. The task now is to test your beliefs. You may examine and question beliefs and faith as you would deal with intense experiences or deep dreams.

Your present challenges require you to have the courage to acknowledge your feelings and to be alert when you act on them.

PAGE/PRINCESS OF CUPS
SPIRITUAL PASSION

Your passions are a clear measure of your inner life like the fish in the Waite-Smith card, which is displayed openly, away from its usual place in and underneath the surface of the water. Your passions shape your feelings. That is what the crystals attached to the gown of the princess imply in the Crowley-Harris card.

Make sure that by crystallizing your feelings you are not turning them into fixations. When isolated, feelings are like a fish out of water. Creative passions keep things moving, building lasting moments and treasures no matter what the changes.

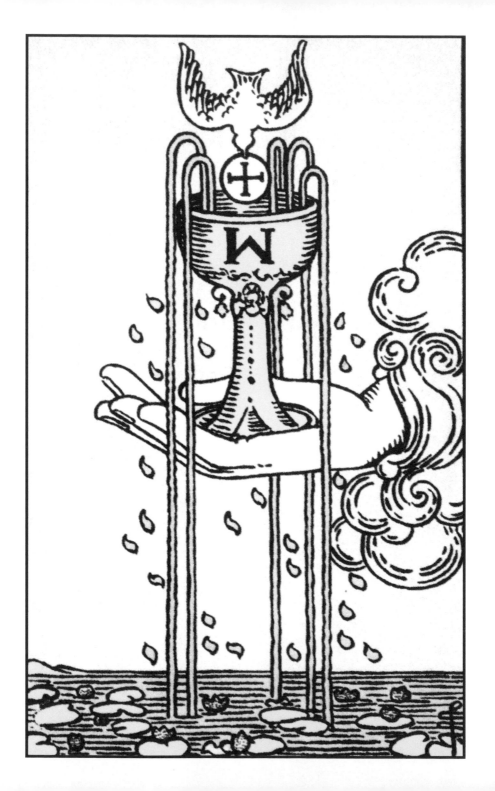

ACE OF CUPS

REBIRTH OF THE SOUL

The Fountain of Youth and the ritual of baptism symbolize
the ability of a person to be reborn. By reentering the world
of the water, we can dissolve the old "I" and connect on a primeval level with all that is alive. This illustrates the point that
the life of each individual is finite, and the certainty of death is
part of life. Reemerging from the water represents the process
of rebirth. We experience a sense of happiness and of libera-
tion when we possess the real self. We relinquish our fixation
on the ego and gain a more eloquent concept of individuality.

    In the context of your present question, consider it a gift
that the water and the cup have been offered to you. This gift
gives your inner, personal life a new starting point, lets you
consciously use your inner powers, and connects you to everything that is alive. You possess your very own special cup. You
are free to find and give fulfillment and satisfaction.

II OF CUPS

TRUE LOVE

How do you experience this card? Every one of us has had a
cup filled with murky, bitter waters. Are we so quick to forget
our psychic pain that we have lost the ability to recognize a
picture of it? Or are we really feeling a lack of love and need
to catch up with an overflow of feelings so that our soul takes
flight? Are we experiencing all of this simply because we want
to see what we long for in the cards? Yet that which seems on
first sight so cheerful can also be an expression of a great deal
of dissatisfaction. One side gives up the cup again and again,
while the other side constantly takes more and more cups.
The head of the lion in the Waite-Smith card and the flowing
waters in the Crowley-Harris card indicate that the unholy
grip we find ourselves caught in could be the result of inner
duress or emotional stress.

   True love helps each participant grow and unfold to
his or her unswerving truth. Each of us must first recognize
and then resolve the dichotomies that are part of all of us.
When we have done so, love will no longer be a substitute for
wholeness and self-fulfillment. We will experience the sheer
delight of being alive and of sharing with others. Now is the
time to begin this journey.

III OF CUPS

NEEDS RESPECTED

Here we are dealing with mixed feelings. The streams of water crossing each other in the Crowley-Harris card and the intertwining of the arms of the figures in the Waite-Smith card make it difficult to determine who is holding which cup.

This conveys a feeling of togetherness that can be very animating and confirming. However, the danger is that we may forget where one individual begins and the other ends. The individual may simply get lost, which also implies mixed feelings. A sense of realism may be setting in, but the possible fruits of the blessing are lying unattended on the ground or are hidden behind the figures (see the right figure in the Waite-Smith card).

The third important element in the Waite-Smith card is that the figure in the foreground has her back turned to the viewer. If we want to experience a full measure of happiness, we must acknowledge the shadowy side of each person. We must each have a chance to reject any side that is personally unacceptable to us. Only when we consider all the essential needs of the participants will happiness and a magical feeling be a natural part of our relationships.

Do not depend on someone else's approval to validate your own feelings. Accept the feelings of others, even if you can't identify with those feelings. Make sure others understand your needs. The right word at the right time will do wonders.

IV OF CUPS

YOUR OWN SENSE

The capacity for expansive emotions is a gift, but this gift can also exhaust you. Sometimes we think our feelings are too strong or that they are responsible for at least some of our disappointments. Yet our experience tells us that we rarely love or feel too much. The problem is that we don't know what to do with our feelings and desires.

Instead of trying to hold back, minimize our emotions, or find new and permanent objects for our love, we must discover the meaning and worth of our own lives. We must allow our essence to be alive, as the image of the tree suggests in the Waite-Smith card.

Trust your feelings. Try to accept the uniqueness of each person. Stop censuring your feelings. Instead, look for their meaning. Accept your likes and dislikes and make them work for you.

V OF CUPS

END OF ILLUSIONS

The black figure in the Waite-Smith deck card reminds us of sadness. In the Crowley-Harris deck, this is the only Cups card in which nothing recognizable flows. Instead, we see the shadowy side of our emotions. This is a serious warning, but it is also an auspicious sign. In any case, the advantage is that the shadows are actually visible.

When one sees everything in black on a card, it is a warning signal. Don't deny it. Decide what frightens you and what disappoints you. Depending upon the situation, pull back or look for help and support; but whatever you do, make sure that you express your feelings. Feel the grief for what you have lost and, if there is still time, do something about it.

The empty cups in the Crowley-Harris card also mean that your emotions are drawing a line through the past and that you are now completely open to a new beginning. That also is the positive meaning of the black figure that appears in some decks. Your soul and feelings are like a mirror. The psyche sees only darkness when there is no picture. Most of all, you can only dimly feel, like intuition, anything that is truly new to the soul. This encounter with your shadow can evoke happy feelings. You have the same sort of feelings when you see the dark outline of the shore for the first time after a long ocean journey. In this case, get ready for the arrival. Look forward to this new psychic shore with joyful anticipation.

interpretations
for each card

VI OF CUPS

FOUNTAIN OF YOUTH

Originally, baptism was a rite in which an adult was submerged in water. When fairy tales speak of the fountain of youth, they often mean the same kind of act: stepping deep into the abyss in order to emerge again psychically as a new person. The cleansing, renewing power of water is a symbol for the soul, granting us rebirth, now and in the future.

The small woman on the right in the Waite-Smith card has two faces. In the center of the picture, she is looking up at the man, facing him. The other face shows the exact opposite: she is turning away, looking down at the ground. Both lines of vision are necessary. Affection and aversion. Sympathy and antipathy. Each part of the pair is needed to keep the inner life flowing because we have become accustomed to a certain emotional behavior and prefer to react with an emotional either/or. The classical meaning of baptism and the secret of the fountain of youth are to dissolve such rigid fixations. The rebirth of the soul means that new alternatives are now available for your emotions. You will learn many different ways for your soul to travel (see Crowley-Harris card). You are experiencing a period when your emotional switch can be reset, as represented by the "X" to the left of the man in the Waite-Smith card. Make use of the hour. Relinquish old fears so that you may fulfill your deepest desires.

*interpretations
for each card*

159

VII OF CUPS

DREAMS LIVED

Here's another turning point in your emotional development. An imaginary, fantastic world is opening up for you. Jump over your own shadow and reach out.

At the same time, you will experience yourself as the dancer in your dreams and as the victim of vacillating fantasies. Put an end to your shadowy existence. The game is over; the performance has come to an end. Give form and color to your existence. Stop playing hide-and-seek.

Your task in this card is to determine which dreams and which fears have true meaning for you. As depicted in the Crowley-Harris card, extraneous expectations and fears have to drip out until only the promises that give a measure of harmony to your personal happiness are left in the cup.

In some situations, the most intense challenge and seemingly unrealistic vision is precisely what you need in order to accomplish the task. In other situations, even the tiniest temptation or the most auspicious promise might spell trouble. Follow those fears or hopes that produce the most powerful emotions and put them into action. Only the results will tell you if they were right for you.

*interpretations
for each card*

161

VIII OF CUPS

GO WITH THE FLOW

The happy options of the eight cups have nothing to do with inertia, but rather with the fact that they follow the supporting and flowing power of the river. "Indolence" is the title for this Crowley-Harris card, which means causing little or no pain, being lazy in the sense of numbness, or having no feelings.

Strangely enough, the pain we experience is relative. If it is very bad, we turn off part of our feelings. Much will then simply pass us by, but the lessening of the pain seems to be worth the price we have to pay for it. But when we follow a compelling vision toward an important goal, the actual pain seems to lose its power. The perception has changed even if the intensity of our feelings has actually increased.

"Faith can move mountains." If you don't believe, hurdles will pile up in front of you. Inertia will set in. Operating from belief helps us consolidate our energies, guiding us like a red sign as indicated by the red figure in the Waite-Smith card.

Don't let your feelings and emotions force you into preconceived logic. On the contrary, let the logic of your soul be the guide for your journey. Don't wait until someone comes to give you a jump start. Set yourself in motion.

IX OF CUPS

EMOTIONAL WEALTH

How do you see yourself? Do you have a lot of fantasies or only a few? Do you seldom dream? If so, you are like the figure in the Waite-Smith card in which many cups are present but they are all behind the figure, in the shadow. Do you dream a lot? The Crowley-Harris card shows a monument of lively feelings and fantasies.

While the figure in the Waite-Smith card has no contact with the cups behind his back, the cups in the Marseilles and Crowley-Harris cards are all interconnected. This could be a problem if one of the cups moves out of position. The relationship between the part and the whole is a difficult one for you. You can relate to "full steam ahead" and "all or nothing." You may have the feeling or the fear that by starting something at a particular place you will set an avalanche in motion. Don't be afraid, and don't try to outshine everybody else. Accept that different truths can exist side by side and that this is not an obstacle as long as both sides are willing to learn from the other. Determine what support you can expect for your needs and what greater understanding you might muster for the needs of other people.

X OF CUPS

CULTIVATE PASSION

This is similar to the "IX–Cups" card. Here, too, it is particularly important that you make the critical distinctions in your emotional and spiritual life. Simply blending together fire and water, feminine and masculine energies, etc. (see the Waite-Smith deck picture) is dangerous, particularly when it comes to inner dependence and external isolation.

The ten cups in the rainbow on the Waite-Smith card represent isolation. In a negative sense, the rainbow acts as a glass bowl or a strong protective shield. The Crowley-Harris card reminds us of an emotional corset, which can be interpreted as personifying the tree of life. In short, because we are afraid of too many feelings, we run the risk of hiding behind rigid formalities or conventional belief systems. The task is to bring grand emotions to a satisfying realization. To do so, we must compose an all-encompassing work of art that shows us standing in the center.

For the actual moment at hand, you must have the courage to show your feelings. Your self-awareness and knowledge of human nature is put to the test. The more you clarify your expectations of yourself and of others, the more the doors to the heavens will be open to you. Don't let others overwhelm you, but remember that others need to be accepted as unique individuals too.

*interpretations
for each card*

Mind · The Weapons of Reason · Intellect · Know-how

SWORDS REPRESENT THE ELEMENT of air. The key principle is the mind. Since ancient times, the sword has personified the power of judgment and the ability to arrive at a verdict and to carry it out.

A sword helps you to penetrate, separate, and define, enabling you to make a decision as well as to gain insight and form concepts. In short, the Tarot Swords are the weapons of the mind, even though we think of swords as tools of war. But wars, too, are inventions of the human mind, and, in their form and extent, they have no other example in nature. If you see an image of fighting and war in the Swords, do not forget chivalry, responsibility, and freedom—their other traditional attributes.

Whenever you pull a Swords card, your task is always to look for clarity, to find a solution, to provide a fresh current, good air, and "strong breath." Other associations with Swords include "swords into plowshares," armor, readiness to attack and defend, toughness, worsening conflict, concepts and consequences, the human condition, and stars. As Shakespeare would tell us, there are more things in heaven and earth than we can imagine. Between heaven and earth there is also air.

*interpretations
for each card*

⋮

QUEEN OF SWORDS

THE SECOND FACE

Now you need a wider perspective, clear judgment, and a good overview. You'll need a clear head and freedom to make decisions as you use your enormous energies and ideas.

Unlike the other Swords Court Cards, here we see a particularly dense layer of clouds between heaven and earth. This is a sign of being one step removed from the unpleasantness and trivialities of everyday events, but it is also a sign of being somewhat remote.

Depending on the circumstances, you can see the latter as a certain strength or coolness and also as a special talent for imagination and creativity. Thanks to your rich imagination, you are able to see things in your mind that others may be totally unaware of. This means that you can look at life intellectually. You are a pioneer in the field of the imagination and often experience moments of almost dreamlike clarity that also make it possible for you to be the victim of false perceptions and incredible conjectures.

Reveal your intelligence. In the Waite-Smith card, the left side of the face is the side of the unconscious, which is still unknown. The Crowley-Harris card points to the task of removing the mask to discover the real face. You must not be misled by a superimposed superego. You are particularly gifted, but you are also dependent on the gift. Discover your real needs and stand up for them without compromise or arrogance.

*interpretations
for each card*

171

KING/PRINCE OF SWORDS

PULLING STRINGS

What is most important for you here is to have perspective, to be farsighted, and to have a good portion of superiority and mental control. While you are acquiring or cultivating an admirable degree of sovereignty, you are also prone to "pulling strings," keeping people and events on a string, preventing them from ever being totally free of your control. You have the talent to convey your ideas and knowledge very effectively, but the boundary between operating by remote control and imperceptibly manipulating others is often very narrow.

The greatest risk is that you may be manipulating yourself and misunderstanding your own true intentions. The sword is leaning to the left side of the card, a symbol of the tendency toward the unconscious. As long as you ignore the unconscious, you will miss your most important possibilities. The motto "What I don't know won't hurt me" is not for you.

Your intellectual activities and the tension you are under are an indirect sign that you are a passionate person. Whether or not you express them, you possess great visions and passions. At the same time, you are capable of organizing your life according to what you believe is right for you. This makes it imperative that you use the weapon of your mind in a way that gives your passions a chance to be conscious and fulfilling.

interpretations
for each card

173

KNIGHT OF SWORDS

RACING THOUGHTS

You won't allow yourself to be forced into a corner. Places, persons, and perspectives change with breathtaking speed. The "Knight of Swords" is moving to the left side of the card, in the direction of the unconscious. Ask yourself what this might mean for you. If your thinking is strictly on an unconscious level, it is wild thinking. When your thoughts follow the chaos of the unconscious, you are a quicker, more imaginative, and livelier thinker than when your thoughts revolve around logic. But in the former you may run the risk of becoming a "ghost rider." Are you someone who loves to go after the unconscious, who does battle with it, searching for a way to get a handle on things? Do you fight the flaws of nature in yourself and against the stupidity of others? In any case, you will always be susceptible to and influenced by either other people or your own impulses. As soon as you become excited, your thoughts are powerfully influenced, just like an electrical coil when it comes near a strong magnet.

To a certain extent, your happiness and well-being depend on how you deal consciously with your unconscious, how you confront and neutralize your shadow side so that a friendship between your conscious and your whole existence can develop.

interpretations
for each card

175

PAGE/PRINCESS OF SWORDS
ADVENTURE OF THE MIND

It will be easier for you to make decisions and your life will get a lift when you get your mind moving and let yourself be inspired by the one mind that is present everywhere.

The zigzag lines of the air in the Crowley-Harris card indicate the effortlessness of your thinking. They signal unconventional, free, and adventurous thinking that could have you tilting at windmills. The windmills indicate a talent for thinking in broad terms or a tendency to get bogged down. The "Page/Princess of Swords" can be a creative event, standing for brainstorming and for the passionate exchange of many different, volatile ideas and associations.

Be aware of superficial engagements and ambiguous efforts. Don't engage in futile fights or allow yourself to be drawn into confrontations. Preserve your easygoing nature, your humor, and your cheerfulness. Trying to understand is what makes life easier. When you live more consciously, life will become more stimulating for you and for the people around you.

ACE OF SWORDS

THE CROWNING OF THE MIND

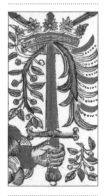

Your mind will only reach full power when you liberate it from all limitations of thought and venture forward into the absolute and the unconditional. That, however, brings with it the danger of being separated from your own roots, from your natural, original state. Only when you connect unconditional consideration to the necessity of your personal existence will your mental abilities bear fruit.

The human mind represents the quintessential crowning of creation, not the plunderer of nature. Therefore, human consciousness is the crowning of the human mind.

Consciousness means being conscious, living and acting consciously. In the Waite-Smith and Crowley-Harris decks, the crown is pictured as a complete circle, representing the oneness of consciousness, the counterbalance to the double-edged sword. For your question, the card is suggesting that you sharpen and increase your awareness so as to better understand contradictions. Pay attention and support oneness and inner congruency of thinking and acting. Free yourself from doubt and duplicity. Life is offering you the sword again, the air and awareness. Accept the gift of awareness. Make use of it so that you may find new solutions and make new decisions for a more worthwhile life lived on a humane earth.

*interpretations
for each card*

II OF SWORDS

A DIFFERENT WAY OF SEEING

Where the obvious ends, the world of the imagination begins.
Give power to creative fantasies. Pay attention to your dreams,
moods, and intuitions. Explore areas that are foreign to you!

The moon and the ocean in the background of the
Waite-Smith card are the borderline of the soul between the
subconscious and the conscious. The same balance of mind
and soul is also present in the Crowley Harris card. The
white flower in the center of the Crowley-Harris card represents your own center. The swords connect the right and
left halves of the body, the right and left side of the brain, and
your emotional and rational side. You should not expect only
peace, as the title of the Crowley-Harris card suggests. Right
now, certain emotions and needs are waiting for clarification
and are calling for a decision. These confrontations are not
always handled peacefully. Vague premonitions are the side
effects of fear, nervousness, and stomachaches. Breathe deeply
to lighten the confrontation. Don't hide behind uncertainty
and ignorance. Begin to interpret your fantasies and dreams.
Which ones catch your attention? How do you see them?
What message do you recognize in them? What are you going
to do with them?

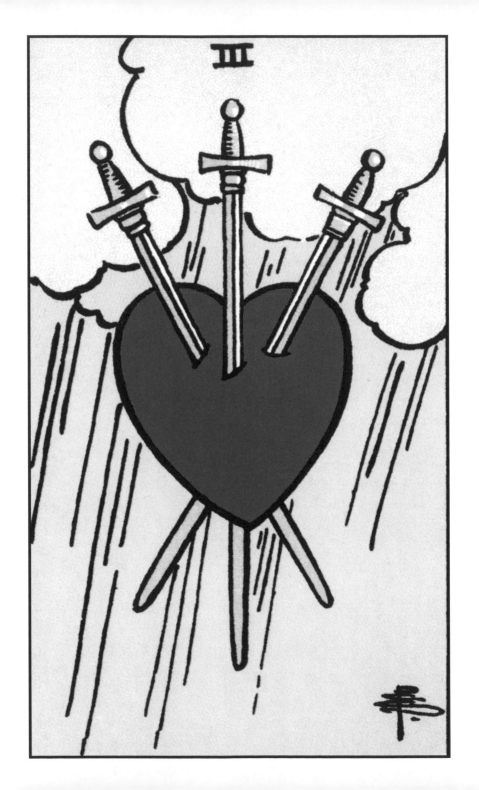

III OF SWORDS

INTERFACE

It is wrong to think that the Swords bring us only grief. The Waite-Smith card shows swords piercing the heart. The heart and the weapons of the mind touch and penetrate here. Two different systems, awareness and the unconscious, mind and emotions, recognition and consternation are coupled and integrated. The hatch marks in the Waite-Smith card mean rain, or they imply a mirror. Pieces of a mirror are also part of the Crowley-Harris card.

Whenever you pull this card, you might as well stop pretending to yourself and to others. This is a very special invitation to begin to explore, name, and express that which is closest to your heart. Express what is moving you. Speak frankly and don't get trapped in love or hate. Worries, pain, rage, revenge, and envy need to be mindfully handled, as do love, joy, passion, and gratitude, among other emotions. Examine your emotions with a critical mind and loving understanding. You'll experience enormous relief when your heart is again free to be the interface for communication and understanding.

IV OF SWORDS

A QUIET MIND

The mind never rests. It is active all the time. Even during sleep it is constantly pouring out images that often find expression in dreams. Only if our mind is alive and undisturbed can it find peace. If it is not filled with worried thoughts, it can do its job undisturbed. Do you need time for solitude or a vacation? Are you ignoring the fact that you need a break? If that is the case, this card tells you that you need one to mobilize your mental capacities so that they are functioning fully again.

In many cases, however, this card refers to inner quiet that brings about personal satisfaction and a sound conscience. The figure on the left in the Waite-Smith card contains the word *PAX*, which means peace. In order to preserve your peace, or to regain it, you might have to be somewhat less careful. Instead of standing back graciously, be more forceful and end your "slumber." The window in the Waite-Smith card and the multifaceted flower in the Crowley-Harris card make it clear that you must use your mental strength and analyze your thoughts and experiences until all the pieces come together like a mosaic. Then you can solve the puzzle.

V OF SWORDS

RESOLVING FEAR

Don't be afraid. Although conventional wisdom says that this card represents malicious boasting and/or defeat, there are many possible meanings.

For instance, the Crowley-Harris card says so much more than its subtitle, "Defeat," implies. True, all five swords are bent and damaged, but they have been used, and you have gained experience because you used them. The swords are connected by drops of blood representing injuries and sorrow, but the weapons of the mind have been directed by life's blood. The drops of blood make up the picture of a Pentagram with the tip pointing to the ground, indicating energy directed downward. This also indicates reconnecting the mind with matter, grounding your awareness and making it fruitful. The swords are facing each other, but they meet in the common center.

The Waite-Smith card also means that the times when you felt small and insignificant are over. In hindsight, you are able to understand and forgive yourself and other people for difficulties, fears, and weaknesses and accept or reject them. "Knowledge without conscience is only half-knowledge." Take care of your worries and fears. Be clear about what you know and accept that which you don't. This will guide you to the quintessential you (represented by the number five or, as in the Crowley-Harris card, by the Pentagram). Quintessential knowledge, however, is dynamic awareness, a personal clarity that is enriching and freeing.

VI OF SWORDS

WORKING TO GET ACROSS THE RIVER

On first sight, the Waite-Smith card implies a move to another place or changes in the environment. But it also represents strength and the job of integrating different worlds. Setting out to cross the river also involves translating from one language to another. The Crowley-Harris card illustrates simultaneously contrasting and unifying different worlds. Self-awareness can express itself in many different and complex ways. Perceptions can come from many different directions, and they can be reduced to one common denominator.

Awareness can be like the boat in the Waite-Smith picture. Whether you can improve the actual situation depends on the clarity and openness of your mind. Nonproductive thoughts can obstruct your view. They are like old baggage that you drag into every new situation. Healthy thinking points the way like a compass needle.

Thinking productively proceeds from what you and/or others want. You will then find the way. That's what the center cross with the roses stands for in the Crowley-Harris card. Healthy thoughts are based on properly understanding a situation, just as the man in the boat in the Waite-Smith card can move along when his pole makes contact with the ground beneath the water. Be thorough when confronting your conflicts. Make use of your mental agility so that you can determine what it is that concerns you and others. Be thorough in bringing your needs to the attention of others.

*interpretations
for each card*

⋮

VII OF SWORDS

FINDING SOLUTIONS

When you know what you know and know what you don't know, you will also understand where you have been and where you want to go. In many ways, your present situation is puzzling and full of conflicts. Deciding what you want and going after it will be helpful in finding the solution you are looking for today.

When you don't want to understand yourself or others, you'll interpret this card as cunning, plotting, foolish, and futile. It will take time to find your own solutions. Many perceptions and influences are working against you. In the Crowley-Harris card, the arrangement of the six small swords contrasted with the one large one expresses conflicting tendencies. In the Waite-Smith card, the figure is a vivid contradiction in itself. What is important here is for you to accept and overcome arguments and uncomfortable opinions from other people. Resourcefulness and staying power are your best weapons.

Examine your understanding of yourself. Every argument you are considering, even those directed against you, will strengthen you. These arguments will help clarify your journey. Your self-knowledge, which is now a small plant, will grow into a tall tree. This is what the seven swords of the Crowley-Harris card represent.

*interpretations
for each card*

VIII OF SWORDS

CONSEQUENCES OF THE INTELLECT

Consequences can take any number of different forms. For instance, at this very moment you feel uncomfortable, you are experiencing confrontations, or you are limited by your present situation. Trivial matters are taking up your time unnecessarily, and you are in danger of missing your chance. It is time to free yourself, to loosen up, and to take more risks. The card is telling you that it is the little things that are standing in your way (see Crowley-Harris card). If you know that your hands are tied but that you have the swords at your disposal, it will be easy to separate yourself from unreasonable restraints and dependencies (see Waite-Smith card). Handle the swords with caution, but cut the chains.

On the other hand, it might not be your difficulties that lead you to examine the effects of your thoughts. You might have reached a new level precisely because of your successes, because of a newfound clarity that requires new thinking and new insights. Some changes in your life can only be accomplished if you understand your thoughts. In that sense, you need a phase of self-examination, a time for thoughtful observation of even the smallest contradiction and of the larger connection. What is needed here is your commitment. You will experience remarkable improvement when you integrate and unify your thoughts with your actions.

*interpretations
for each card*

193

IX OF SWORDS

COMPREHEND THE
INCOMPREHENSIBLE

This card is often interpreted as the station of despair, of
nightmares, etc. That is understandable, since this is one of
the meanings of the Waite-Smith card. The swords in the
Crowley-Harris card, still dripping with blood, also invoke all
kinds of horror. *Cruelty* is the title of the Crowley-Harris card.
As always, the title represents only one small aspect of this
particular card.

As far as the connection between swords and blood
in the Crowley-Harris card is concerned, we might want to
compare it to a similar theme in the card "III–Swords" from
the Waite-Smith deck. If our thoughts go directly to what is in
our blood and what is truly in our heart, we run the danger
of shortchanging the connection between our heart and our
intellect. Behavior dictated by such a knee-jerk reaction is
implied by the title of the Crowley-Harris card. On the other
hand, a direct connection between the external and internal
worlds, between the heart and the intellect, can be enormously
favorable and can provide great clarity. You are finally able to
understand what your thoughts mean. That which moves your
soul will allow you to find clear, conscious, and diverse forms
of expression. Congratulations!

The Waite-Smith card depicts the same process. You are
beginning to grasp the consequences and the meaning of your
thoughts. Light is penetrating darkness, and you are beginning
to understand many things that have been a puzzle to you.
That is cause for great joy. Get used to your new intellectual
horizon slowly.

X OF SWORDS

FRUITS OF THE MIND

Here, unhealthy thoughts and fruitless confrontations are condemned. The swords depicted in the Crowley-Harris card are partially damaged, and some of the tips are broken off. This also means that the swords were needed and have been used. They have done their duty. The grips of the swords in the same picture represent the ten stations of the Tree of Life of Qabalah. In other words, they are a symbol of wholeness, a culmination of the thought process. You can now harvest the fruits of the mind.

If you want to know if your thoughts and theories are correct, you must allow them to help you. Only when using them becomes second nature to you and becomes anchored to your whole existence can the seeds of the intellect bear fruit. Tarot does not use the image of either a wise man or a wise woman to represent the fullness of mental powers. Rather, the flower of insight begins to unfold when you cease identifying with an ideal or a role model. In a positive sense, the swords are clearing the way so that you may open yourself to life, and be unhindered, free of preconceived notions, but aware and consistent.

Body · Finance · Values · Talents

PENTACLES/DISKS

THE PENTACLES/DISKS represent the element of earth. The key concept is body, which refers to the human body as well as to all physical matter. Whenever you pull a Pentacles/Disks card, the issues are the practical results you find, change, or produce yourself.

The term *talent* has great importance here. Even in biblical times, talent was a coin. Material and financial definitions always come to mind when referring to Pentacles/Disks. These are also connected to the word *talent*. At the same time, Pentacles/Disks also imply defining and creating. We become aware of how different circumstances have defined or are still defining us. We also see how we define ourselves and the world around us. In a way, the Pentacles/Disks become the mirror of our handicaps, our tasks, and our abilities. This deeper meaning of Pentacles/Disks is also expressed through the word *talent*.

When Crowley-Harris created his version of the Tarot cards, he changed the name *pentacles* to *disks*, because he wanted to create "an image of turning and whirling." The concept of the Pentacles/Disks as something active is also evident in the cards of the other Tarot decks. The Pentagram in the Waite-Smith deck expresses the active energies that are part of every fact. Indeed, even the traditional Pentacles in the Marseilles deck, with their gold and black colors, introduce an active interplay of light and shadow.

Other associations relevant to Pentacles/Disks include the face and weight of Earth, and the interplay and constant feedback between what we accomplish and that which defines us. We can learn who and what we are if we discover the meaning of our changing talents, if we find gold that, on first sight, looks just like a simple rock.

*interpretations
for each card*

⋮

199

QUEEN OF PENTACLES/DISKS

RECOGNIZING THE ESSENTIAL

The "Queen of Pentacles/Disks" represents the power that
you possess to create peak experiences. In the Waite-Smith
and Crowley-Harris cards, this is represented by the symbol
of the mountain goat whose home is the symbolic place where
heaven and earth meet. The close link between spirit and
matter, between human and the universe, as well as between
hard reality and lofty independence is, therefore, also part of
your world. The blue mountains of the Waite-Smith card and
the desert of the Crowley-Harris card represent your ability to
accept and deal with the difficulties in your life.

Protect yourself against feelings of self-importance and
low self-esteem. Cultivate that which you cherish most. Don't
brag about what is special about you. Each human being is a
unique product of nature. Love that which is alive in you and
in the people around you. Paying attention to reality will give
you the answers to what is most significant at this point. If you
hold on to those ideas, you will always be at the height of your
possibilities. Is there such a thing as permanent happiness?

KING OF PENTACLES/ PRINCE OF DISKS

SENSE AND PLEASURE

Working to earn money and spending money in order to enjoy it make up the two halves of the loaf according to the symbolic meaning of the "King of Pentacles" or "Prince of Disks." They stand for the affinity that exists between work and pleasure and between sense and passion.

The grapes in the Waite-Smith and Crowley-Harris cards introduce the images of wine and the vineyard. Wine literally means the sweetness of life and its truth ("in vino veritas"). The pleasure of being elevates sense and passion. At the same time, note that the vineyard is a symbol of the hard work needed to cultivate the earth and to harvest the fruit.

The steer in the Waite-Smith card points to the astrological sign of Taurus, whose main month is May. May offers such an alluring promise in which everything is created anew, but only the Taurus knows how much responsibility can be hidden in the "everything." What a task! The cards show how much hard work has to be done and how heavy the stones are that need to be moved in order to build a life. But while you are doing your work, no one is more content and self-composed than you!

*interpretations
for each card*

203

KNIGHT OF PENTACLES/DISKS

CHAFF AND WHEAT

Pentacles/Disks are a symbol of your dowry, your possessions, and your material possibilities with all their advantages and disadvantages. You will discover what your real talents are, what is and isn't productive in your life, when you correct avoidable mistakes and stop sweeping the blunders that are inevitable under the rug. Instead, you must use them to fertilize the fields of life and the garden of experience.

Johannes Tauler, a medieval German mystic, used the following analogy: "A horse does its 'business' in its stall. But then the same horse expends great effort to pull a cart filled with the manure out to the fields. The golden wheat and sweet grapes could not grow in the fields without it."

Now, in this context, the mess represents the shortcomings that you can neither ignore, overcome, nor put aside. Carry them with great care to God's field of love. Scatter your "manure" across this precious field, and from it will grow the most splendid, wonderful "fruit."

Don't be afraid of disagreements that make you feel uncomfortable. If your own and other people's "manure" is that useful, how much more beneficial will your talents be!

PAGE OF PENTACLES/
PRINCESS OF DISKS

TESTING YOUR TALENTS

This card tells you that you have a wonderful opportunity to rediscover and reevaluate your practical skills. Ashes (carbon) and diamonds are made up of the same combination of chemicals, and in this sense, they are identical. But the different pressures they were exposed to in the earth brought about very different results. The same is true for your practical talents and skills. Certain stressful situations will help develop new skills, while others lose their importance.

The inconspicuous also hides the conspicuous, the essential, and the typical. That is important now. Test your values and your value system. By redefining what is essential and what is inconsequential, you are elevating the gold that was lying in the street (see Marseilles card) and seizing your diamond (see Crowley-Harris card). Your inner wealth now has new value.

ACE OF PENTACLES/DISKS

THE SPIRIT OF THE COIN

Everything has two sides. That gives ambiguity to every-thing—every matter and every question. Now is the time to take the material contradictions into your hands. You will be able to identify and use the tension, which is potential energy, in every situation.

Human nature is double-rooted. We are citizens of two worlds. The Waite-Smith card suggests the two homes, one heavenly and one earthly, with the double circle of the Pentacle and by its placement right between the top and the bottom. Humans are "big animals," as the Greek inscription around the Disk in the Crowley-Harris card indicates. The animal, both wild and domesticated, within ourselves may represent our instincts as well as our unconscious impulses and automatic habits. These are our animal resources. Clearing them is highly valuable. Sometimes, we need to say good-bye to some "primitive" practices that turn out to be useless or delusional. Sometimes, though, we get in touch anew with deep, primordial, and original sources both within ourselves and others.

Use this card as a chance to reevaluate the weight and value of your unique existence. Discover anew what the world has to offer you and what you have to offer the world.

*interpretations
for each card*

209

II OF PENTACLES/DISKS
PERSONAL CONNECTION

New facts, values, and events are moving to the forefront in
your present situation. These have always been present and
always been possible, but now they make themselves known
and assume particular importance.

You question old habits. Your awareness is shifting,
and you are discovering new beliefs that gain importance in
your life. Your self-image and your ego are being jarred and
given impetus.

Don't let yourself be alarmed. It is like being on a roller
coaster: the changes between the highs and the lows are strongest in the beginning, but the longer you stay on the ride, the
more natural they become.

Take note of your contribution to the changes that are
taking place. Avoid thinking that the changes are a coinci-
dence or that they are accidental. Instead, see the connection.
Be aware of and insist on a connection. Your strength allows
you to sort out and bring together the different aspects at play.
Roll up your sleeves!

III OF PENTACLES/DISKS

NEW BELIEFS

In the Waite-Smith deck, this card depicts images of work and wages. We all have untapped talents. Now you show what you've got. Let yourself be surprised by what others have to offer. Michelangelo is supposed to have said that the sculptor (see Waite-Smith card) puts nothing into the stone. He only frees the figure trapped inside by the burdens surrounding it. Throw away your burden! Cultivate your energies and your efforts!

Let the light shine on new skills to uncover the essentials concerning your present question. Bury old, unproductive habits. Create new results and peak experiences. Show them what you can do with what you've got.

IV OF PENTACLES/DISKS

UNDERSTAND YOUR TALENTS

The squares in the Crowley-Harris and Marseilles cards point
to the four elements, the corners of the world. Confronted
by the whole universe, you can and must give witness to your
essential self and verify the value of your talents.

Build up your talents. You discover them when you
understand how life has molded your skills and handicaps.
What meets your needs and your desires? What is useful
to others?

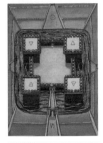

One side of the medal (pentacle, disk) is the question:
What "coined" you? The other side of it says: What will you
establish? How will you design and coin your contribution to
the world?

Don't play the role of the hero or the loser. Say good-bye
to bragging and moral cowardice. Your strengths and your
weaknesses have special value. Choose and create a framework in which your values and your existence are rewarded.

V OF PENTACLES/DISKS

SHARING IS CARING

Hard-heartedness, trouble, and pain are to some extent self-made. If you want to end or change a bad situation, you simply need to accept certain characteristics in yourself and in others. Strengthen your talents. Weakness, too, has its worth and grace. Be considerate and remember that not everyone grows at the same rate. Make a difference. Don't compare apples with oranges.

On the other hand, worry and misery are neither completely self-made nor a punishment of fate—they are part of the state of the human existence. With this in mind, the message of this card is to share personal distress and thereby resolve it. A legend tells of two people who are making the same journey. One is lame, and the other is blind. The blind one supports the lame one, and the lame one leads the blind one. By sharing their handicaps, they are freed from their respective helplessness. We multiply individual strength when we work together.

VI OF PENTACLES/DISKS

REALIZED NEEDS

Make your needs known and be open to the needs of others.
When you do this, your love and your self-esteem will blos-
som. Your current practical question will be successfully
answered when you understand that your desires, just like
your talents, are your fortune.

When giving and taking are in balance, two outcomes
are possible. On the one hand, nothing essential will happen.
The scale does not move because no weight is exchanged.
On the other hand, the scale may remain in balance because
everyone involved gains equally. If we can establish real
needs and deeds, those who give and those who receive will
be winners.

If you satisfy other people's needs by using your talents,
and if your needs awaken and further other people's talents,
then each participant will be a winner at the same time. Make
sure that you are not simply managing or making do but that
you are striving for personal gain and common benefit.

This newly created wealth is represented by the four
small coins that appear in the air between the larger and
smaller figures. This kind of a mutual gain is a blessing. The
right-hand fingers of the big person here resemble the blessing
of the main figure of the card "V–The High Priest."

*interpretations
for each card*

VII OF PENTACLES/DISKS
PERSONAL STANDARD

The figure in the Waite-Smith card is wearing two different shoes, implying that it makes a difference if you see a situation in general terms or from your own perspective. Your personal point of view, which is immediately in front of your feet, makes a great deal of difference. You will develop and gain a personal perspective if you assert your own approach rather than follow the path of the past. As far as your present questions are concerned, you can expect the greatest success if you carefully test your own standards against those of others and come to a careful, independent judgment. What might look like failure at first glance can turn out to be worthwhile after all.

Be less dependent on what you and others believe. Instead, trust actual experiences. Find out how you are truly seeing things differently from others. You are confronted with a chance to reevaluate your talents and to complete important tasks.

VIII OF PENTACLES/DISKS

MASTERY

Paradoxically you must grow beyond yourself in order to find yourself. You are now asked to make a contribution to an important situation. Find a new way of seeing your personal tasks and needs. The secret of mastery is to develop your personal talents. Define your essence, your logic, and your truth. Stop being so stubborn, so that your sense of the self blossoms and your senseless habits die. Each situation you master is like a mirror of the work you have done on yourself. The clearer you are about your talents and limitations, the more you will become the master of your own fate. Make sure that you design every success and that each success has your signature.

IX OF PENTACLES/DISKS

NECESSITIES UNDERSTOOD

Your presence in the world makes a difference. You have brought something into the world that enriches it. Therefore, don't hide your light and your beauty! Be generous and show the people around you the kind of treasures you have to give and remember that you yourself are a treasure.

If you want people to notice your inner treasures, you must express them in both the large and small things in life. First, however, you will discover that some habits exist without any thought on your part, and some of these are not to your liking. You must, therefore, take charge of your own life and give it form and your personal stamp. This work is similar to the hard work that has to be accomplished in the vineyards. But the result of your troubles is like a superior wine. In wine there is truth, and you must make your own truth fruitful.

X OF PENTACLES/DISKS

TALENTS IN BLOOM

The ten yellow Pentacles/Disks in the Waite-Smith and Crowley-Harris cards represent the ten stations of the "Tree of Life" of the Qabalah. Like the signs of the zodiac in astrology, this tree is a model for wholeness, unity, and completion. However, what is missing in these cards is the connecting path that creates the shape of the "tree." Complete but unconnected. That is the description of the Tree of Life and of your present situation as well.

Everything is present in the Waite-Smith card: child, adult, old man, humans, animals, culture and civilization, home and far away, and much more. The question is whether you can connect all that you are, all your many skills, and still be able to recognize a piece of yourself in everything that is human without always thinking that everyone must agree with you. Curiously enough, individuality is not possible when going at it alone. Once you find the bridge that connects what is foreign and different in you to others, loneliness disappears just as the fear of being swallowed up by the masses will disappear. Loneliness is actually the shadow of missing individuality.

TAROT
and astrology

THE CONCRETE VISION

Pointing to the card of the "IX–The Hermit" (see p. 81), Brigitte exclaims enthusiastically, "Now I have a totally different picture of astrological signs." Indeed, the Tarot card she is pointing to represents Virgo. "For the longest time, I did not understand what the name *Virgin* meant," she continued. "We are not dealing with a young woman. Even the image of sexual virginity does not play a role. And I have found the solution," she says, pointing to the white base under the feet of "IX–The Hermit" in the Waite-Smith card. "The virgin has something to do with the fact that we are to bring about a state of virginity to the earth. Christians call it paying for original sin, and the Hindus say that we must work on our karma without creating a new one!"

Brigitte has been involved with astrology since she studied psychology, but never with Tarot cards. The combination of astrology and Tarot has opened up a whole new dimension for her. "The strength of astrology is that it deals in concepts. Nothing describes the grammar of the unconscious better than astrology. But since astrology does not use visual images, Tarot cards are a very important addition to it."

PICTURES: FOOD FOR THE SOUL

Each astrological sign and each planet has a specific Tarot card. For instance, for the astrological moon, the individual arena of the soul and the unconscious, the card is "II–The High Priestess." For Neptune and Pisces, the essence of the collective unconscious, one of the respective cards is "XVIII–The Moon." The meaning of this card is the return of something that has been suppressed. Ancient instincts, far-reaching visions, and grand dreams take shape here. The absence of a human figure in this card warns against self-denial and losing touch with reality. In any case, it is a card that encourages us to open our hearts and to stop being intimidated.

We, the authors, have Neptune in Libra, as do all people born between 1942 and 1956. We don't have to relinquish the interpretation of this constellation and what it means in practical terms to astrological recipe books whose interpretive formulas are problematic. The Tarot card for Neptune, "XVIII–The Moon," tells us more. Unsettling as a night with a full moon, all the highs and lows of existence come to the fore, and the Libra within us can lose its balance. But "XVIII–The Moon" also says that strangers become friends. This Tarot card addresses the possibility of forgiveness.

THE MOON.

FIND YOUR STAR

Combining tarot and astrology uses the factors they have in common. The themes of their symbolic languages are quite different, but their goals are not. When you truly deal with your dreams, everything that has been a problem and everything that you have longed for becomes clear.

If you follow your star, you will find yourself in the proper place and on the right path. The greatest challenge is to recognize your own star. This is the same in astronomy. Sometimes, after scientists discover a new star, a reexamination of old photos reveals that this new star was visible, but no one had noticed it. Similarly, we all carry our "own star," our own, personal truth, but more often then not, we are not aware of it. In order for us to recognize this existing star, we need to view familiar connections in a new context.

The symbolic languages of Tarot and astrology provide practical and imaginative aids for finding one's own star. Both ask about the quality of the present, about the chances and the tasks relevant at a certain moment. Just as astrology examines character and modes of behavior, so does Tarot with its many different, traditional, and archetypal images. Love, death, the devil, happiness, trouble, and both the big and little secrets of life are presented in descriptive pictures. While astrology communicates the concepts of personal individualities, Tarot provides a particular view of them. In Tarot, it is the evidence, the self-awareness provided by the Tarot symbols, the immediate dialogue between the picture and the person viewing it, that lead to one's personal "star." At this point, you truly see yourself and your worth. All the problems, contradictions, and ambiguities become clear.

The relationship between Tarot and astrology is particularly apparent when we look to our star for guidance in our life's journey. This explains why Tarot and astrology have only recently been connected. After all, the concept of choosing one's own journey is a rather new idea for most of us.

Astrology originated several thousand years ago. By contrast, Tarot only dates back about 550 years. The connection between the two was not recognized until the second half of the nineteenth century. The Order of the Golden Dawn combined the two symbolic languages, and their conclusions are still accepted today.

This Order of the Golden Dawn was part of the Rosicrucian movement in England. The Tarot cards used most widely, the Waite-Smith and Crowley-Harris decks, were originated by Pamela Colman Smith and Arthur E. Waite, and by Lady Frieda Harris and Aleister Crowley, respectively, all of whom were members of the Order of the Golden Dawn. The creators of both decks followed the basic astrological classification of the Golden Dawn order. We often see these classifications in the cards themselves. For instance, the sign of Aries is found in "IV–The Emperor" in the Waite-Smith deck. The Crowley-Harris deck also uses these classifications extensively.

HOW IT'S DONE

On the following page, you will find a table of the six Tarot cards
that belong to each astrological sign. Which of the astrological
signs are you most interested in today? Take the six relevant cards
out of the deck and look at them carefully. Together, the six make
up one image of the respective astrological sign.

Each six cards create a tension vital for an understanding
of the astrological sign. For example, "IV–The Emperor" and
"XVI–The Tower" are two of the six cards that belong with
Aries. Consider the tension between these two cards. Think about
the contradiction of establishing and tearing down power and
the tension between masculine energy and feminine energy in
"IV–The Emperor" and the "Queen of Wands." Scorpio presents another good example. Notice the contradiction between
death and rebirth, the principle of "passing away and becoming"
in the figure of "XIII–Death" and "XX–Judgement" (The Aeon).
In Gemini, there is tension between the magic of love in "I–The
Magician" and "VI–The Lovers" and the challenges of "VIII, IX,
and X Swords."

Laying out these six cards, just once or again and again, can
be very worthwhile. Meditate on the cards of your astrological
sign. They will have a new message for you every time.

THE TOWER.

DATE	ASTROLOGICAL SIGN	MAJOR CARD	COURT CARD
3/21–4/20	Aries	IV– The Emperor	Queen of Wands
4/21–5/20	Taurus	V– The Hierophant	King of Pentacles (Prince of Disks)
5/21–6/21	Gemini	VI– The Lovers	Knight of Swords
6/22–7/22	Cancer	VII– The Chariot	Queen of Cups
7/23–8/22	Leo	VIII– Strength (XI–Lust)	King of Wands (Prince of Wands)
8/23–9/22	Virgo	IX– The Hermit	Knight of Pentacles (Knight of Disks)
9/23–10/22	Libra	XI–Justice (VIII– Adjustment)	Queen of Swords
10/23–11/21	Scorpio	XIII– Death	King of Cups (Prince of Cups)
11/22–12/20	Sagittarius	XIV– Temperance (Art)	Knight of Wands
12/21–1/19	Capricorn	XV– The Devil	Queen of Pentacles (Queen of Disks)
1/20–2/18	Aquarius	XVII– The Star	King of Swords (Prince of Swords)
2/19–3/20	Pisces	XVIII– The Moon	Knight of Cups

NUMBERED CARDS	SUPPLEMENTAL MAJOR CARD	PLANET
II–IV Wands	XVI–The Tower	Mars
V–VII Pentacles/ V–VII Disks	III–The Empress	Venus
VIII–X Swords	I–Magician (The Magus)	Mercury
II–IV Cups	II–The High Priestess	Moon
V–VII Wands	XIX–The Sun	Sun
VIII–X Pentacles/ VIII–X Disks	I–The Magician (The Magus)	Mercury
II–IV Swords	III–The Empress	Venus
V–VII Cups	XX–Judgement (The Aeon)	Pluto
VIII–X Wands	X–Wheel of Fortune (Fortune)	Jupiter
II–IV Pentacles/ II–IV Disks	XXI–The World (The Universe)	Saturn
V–VII Swords	XXII/0–The Fool	Uranus
VIII–X Cups	XII–The Hanged Man	Neptune

NOTE: In astrology, the sun and the moon are considered planets. The Queen reigns over the minor cards II–IV of her suit, the King/Prince over the cards V–VII, and the Knight VIII–X. The names in parentheses are those of the Crowley deck.

One astrological sign has been assigned to each six-card set. For instance, the cards for Virgo are "IX–The Hermit," "I–The Magician," "Knight of Pentacles/Disks," and "VIII, IX, and X–Pentacles/Disks." The planets assigned to the Minor Arcana are listed in the last column. For example, "XVI–The Tower" is assigned to Mars, "III–The Empress" to Venus, and "I–The Magician" to Mercury.

INDEX

ABOUT THE AUTHORS

Evelin Bürger and Johannes Fiebig have written more than twenty tarot books, which have reached a circulation of over two million copies and have been translated into more than a dozen languages. Since the early 1980s, many standards of contemporary tarot have been introduced by Bürger and Fiebig. They highlight their experience and understanding of the cards as "mirrors of perception" (awareness of the respective focus of view, affectedness, intentions, blind spots, and so on) that reflect the common and individual ways of perception in everyday life.

Fiebig and Bürger founded the German publisher Königsfurt Verlag in 1989, which became the foundation of the current Königsfurt-Urania and AGM-Urania publishing companies. They have two adult children and live close to the city of Kiel at the Baltic Sea, Germany. See also www.fiebig-und-buerger.de.